John Mirk

Instructions for Parish Priests

John Mirk

Instructions for Parish Priests

ISBN/EAN: 9783337429348

Printed in Europe, USA, Canada, Australia, Japan

Cover: Foto ©Lupo / pixelio.de

More available books at **www.hansebooks.com**

Early English Text Society.

Instructions for Parish Priests

By

John Myrc.

... COTTON MS. CLAUDIUS A. II.,

BY

... PEACOCK, F.S.A., &c.

... EARLY E...
... CO., 60, PATE...

MDCCCLXVIII.

Price Four Shillings.

Instructions for Parish Priests

By

John Myrc.

FROM COTTON MS. CLAUDIUS A. II.,

BY

— PEACOCK, F.S.A., &c.

LONDON:
R THE EARLY ENGLI
NER & CO., 60, PATERN

MDCCCLXVIII.

Price Four Shillings.

Early English Text Society.

COMMITTEE OF MANAGEMENT:

DANBY P. FRY, ESQ.
FREDERICK J. FURNIVALL, ESQ.
FITZEDWARD HALL, ESQ.
REV. J. RAWSON LUMBY.
RICHARD MORRIS, ESQ.
H. T. PARKER, ESQ.
REV. GEORGE G. PERRY.
REV. WALTER W. SKEAT.
HENRY B. WHEATLEY, Esq.

(With power to add Workers to their number.)

HONORARY SECRETARY:

HENRY B. WHEATLEY, ESQ., 53, BERNERS STREET, LONDON, W.

BANKERS:

THE UNION BANK OF LONDON, REGENT STREET BRANCH, 14, ARGYLL PLACE, W.

The Publications for the first three years, 1864, 1865, and 1866, are out of print, but a separate subscription has been opened for their immediate reprint, and when thirty additional names have been received, the Texts for 1864 will be sent to press. Subscribers who desire all or either of these years should send their names at once to the Hon. Secretary.

The Publications for 1864 are :—

1. EARLY ENGLISH ALLITERATIVE POEMS, ab. 1320-30 A.D., ed. R. MORRIS.
2. ARTHUR, ab. 1440, ed. F. J. FURNIVALL.
3. LAUDER ON THE DEWTIE OF KYNGIS, ETC., 1556, ed. F. HALL.
4. SIR GAWAYNE AND THE GREEN KNIGHT, ab. 1320-30, ed. R. MORRIS.

The Publications for 1865 are :—

5. HUME'S ORTHOGRAPHIE AND CONGRUITIE OF THE BRITAN TONGUE, ab. 1617, ed. H. B. WHEATLEY.
6. LANCELOT OF THE LAIK, ab. 1500, ed. Rev. W. W. SKEAT.
7. GENESIS AND EXODUS, ab. 1250, ed. R. MORRIS.
8. MORTE ARTHURE, ab. 1440, ed. Rev. G. G. PERRY.
9. THYNNE ON CHAUCER'S WORKS, ab. 1598, ed. Dr. KINGSLEY.
10. MERLIN, ab. 1450, Part I., ed. H. B. WHEATLEY.
11. LYNDESAY'S MONARCHE, ETC., 1552, Part I., ed. F. HALL.
12. THE WRIGHT'S CHASTE WIFE, ab. 1462, ed. F. J. FURNIVALL.

The Publications for 1866 are :—

13. SEINTE MARHERETE, 1200-1330, ed. Rev. O. COCKAYNE.
14. KYNG HORN, FLORIS AND BLANCHEFLOUR, ETC., ed. Rev. J. R. LUMBY.
15. POLITICAL, RELIGIOUS, AND LOVE POEMS, ed. F. J. FURNIVALL.
16. THE BOOK OF QUINTE ESSENCE, ab. 1460-70, ed. F. J. FURNIVALL.
17. PARALLEL EXTRACTS FROM 29 MSS. OF PIERS PLOWMAN, ed. Rev. W. W. SKEAT.
18. HALI MEIDENHAD, ab. 1200, ed. Rev. O. COCKAYNE.
19. LYNDESAY'S MONARCHE, ETC., Part II., ed. F. HALL.
20. HAMPOLE'S ENGLISH PROSE TREATISES, ed. Rev. G. G. PERRY.
21. MERLIN, Part II. ed. H. B. WHEATLEY.
22. PARTENAY OR LUSIGNEN, ed. Rev. W. W. SKEAT.
23. DAN MICHEL'S AYENBITE OF INWYT, 1340, ed. R. MORRIS.

A few copies are left of No. 5, Hume's Orthographie, 4s.; No. 17, Extracts from Piers Plowman, 1s.; No. 20, Hampole's Treatises, 2s.; No. 22, Partenay, 6s.; No. 23, Ayenbite, 10s. 6d.

The Society's Report, January, 1867, with Lists of Texts to be published in future years, etc. etc., can be had on application to the Hon. Secretary, HENRY B. WHEATLEY, Esq., 53, Berners Street, W.

Early English Text Society.

Report of the Committee, January, 1868.

UNEXAMPLED as had been the progress of the Society in former years, its success in the year just passed must be held to have exceeded that of all previous ones, for not only have its own members increased by a hundred and seventy, not only has its income risen to £941, but it has given birth to what are, in fact, four other Societies, namely, its own Extra Series, the Spenser Society, the Roxburghe Library, and the Chaucer Society.* Thus reinforced, the Society can proceed with fresh vigour to the accomplishment of its task, with the determination not to rest till Englishmen shall be able to say of their Early Literature, what the Germans can now say with pride of theirs, "every work of it's printed, and every word of it's glossed." 'England must no longer be content to lag behind. But many a year of strenuous effort lies between this task just begun and its end. It is an effort in which every member of the Society is called on to take part; and during this present year, and all future ones, the Committee rely on its volunteers to put it in possession of, at least, the money power that the Government supplies to its English regulars under the Master of the Rolls,—a thousand a year. With an income of that amount, a real impression could be made on the work before us, and if every Member will but get one fresh subscriber during the year,† the income wanted will be at once secured. To the resolute Members who have made the Society what, in numbers and income, it is, the Committee especially appeal to continue their exertions, so that the Subscribers may be raised to the required thousand.

---

* The collection of Early French Texts, undertaken by MM. Paul Meyer and Gaston Paris, is also mainly due to the Society's example. A Lydgate Society, to take Lydgate, Occleve, and Hawes, is still wanted.

† "I will undertake to get twenty subscribers during 1868. I wish all the rest would undertake to get ten."—John Leigh, Manchester.

The review of the past year's work shows two sides to it; one of much encouragement, the other of less. To take the latter first. Members were offered thirty-two Texts during the year, in the original series, if they would find money for them; they found it only for seven,—and these instead of eleven, as in 1866, —which made necessary the starting of an Extra Series,* but yet that has been only able to take one Text, and part of another. Members were asked to double the Society's income: they left it at its old amount,† only making up by fresh subscriptions for the old revenue from back Texts. They were asked to reprint the back Texts of 1864 and 1865; they have only raised enough to reprint those of 1864. Still, new members take time and trouble to obtain; and that so many were obtained as 170, is cause for congratulation, not complaint. The Society's numbers were in its first three years successively, 145, 260, 409: in 1867 they reached 580; its income was in its first three years successively, £152, £384, £681: in 1867, it was £941; its issues of Texts were, successively, in 1864,-5,-6, four, seven, eleven: in 1867, nine,‡ and this with the help of the Extra Series; but as £68 of the cost of the Ayenbite, published in 1866, was carried over to 1867, in which year that sum (with the money paid for copying MSS. for 1868, etc.,) would have produced one more Text, the issues of 1866 and 1867 may be looked on as equal. Thus, while in numbers (by the help of the Percy folio), and in income (by the help of the Extra Series) the Society has largely increased during 1867, in Texts it may be considered as having maintained its issue of 1866. Moreover, it has, by the establishment of the Extra Series§ for re-editions, taken these out of the way of the Manuscript work for the original Series, that pioneer work which is the Society's most important business.

The Texts of the past year have yielded to no prior ones in interest and importance, as will be manifest when their names are mentioned; they have touched more nearly the life of the people than ever before. In our *Miscellaneous Class*, Mr. Toulmin

---

* The Subscriptions to the Extra Series were at first made due every 1st of June. They are now made due every 1st of January, in order to avoid the necessity of two audits, and to suit the Hon. Secretary's accounts; but those subscribers who find it more convenient to pay their second guinea on June 1st can of course so pay it.

† That is, considering only the original series, for out of the £941 of 1867, the Camden and Philological Societies paid £93, and the Extra Series, £161.

‡ Or reckoning by pages, the issues were in 1864, 481 pages; in 1865, 950 pages; in 1866, 2034 pages; in 1867 there will be about 1860 pages.

§ Mr. Furnivall's letter last June, proposing this Extra Series, has been misunderstood by some as leaving the issue of the Series doubtful. That was not its intention. It meant to say 'The Series *will* be issued. Will you help it?'

Smith's *English Gilds** will cast a light, as long desired as unexpected, on the condition of our early "common and middling folks" (*Gilds*, p. 178) in towns, and show the whole of urban England covered with brotherhoods "for cherishing love and charity among themselves" (p. 184), for mutual help in sickness and old age, and the performance of the last offices to the dead. It is in the spirit of these men that the Editor, Mr. Toulmin Smith, has thrown his work, gratis, into the Society's series, removing it from that superintended by the Master of the Rolls, where the circulation of the book, and its consequent usefulness, would have been lessened, though the Editor's full pay would have been secured. The Committee desire to express their strong sense of this generosity on Mr. Toulmin Smith's part.

The next great work of the year falls also into the *Miscellaneous Class*, for it is in its social aspect rather than its religious, that the Committee regard *The Vision of William concerning Piers Plowman*, as being of importance. For the first time, the first sketch of this noble English Poem has been given to the world, and with a loving care that has never been heretofore bestowed on the later versions. *Pierce the Ploughman's Crede* has likewise been issued under Mr. Skeat's editing, and here again for the first time, have appeared from the MS. the writer's own lines on the Real Presence, altered by the first printer, and copied from him by subsequent editors. For the Extra Series, Mr. Morris's other engagements have not allowed him to produce yet the first part of *Chaucer's Prose Works*, but it will be issued during 1868 to the subscribers to that series for 1867, and the edition will be the only separate one of the poet's prose ever published.

In our second class, Works illustrating our Dialects and the History of our Language, we have not only started our *Dictionary Series*, by the new edition of the first printed English Rhyming Dictionary, rendered now for the first time easily available by Mr. Wheatley's careful Index; but we have in the *English Gilds*, a most important collection of documents of one and the same date, from many of the counties of England, enabling us — under Mr. Richard Morris's guidance—to contrast their varying provincialisms, and also to see the differences between the language of the educated cleric and the provincial scribe of the same town. The linguistic importance of the volume is almost equal to its social, and had it done no more than confirm the existence in Lynn† of the initial x forms

---

* This will, it is hoped, be ready in February, or March.

† The *Songs and Carols* edited by Mr. Thomas Wright, for the Warton Club, in

known also in Coventry and Lincolnshire, it would have justified its publication. It ranks also as the second of our dated Texts (Report, 1866), the *Ayenbite* being the first.

In our third class, *Religious Treatises*, Mr. Perry has given us the nervous and rythmical Sermon that Dan John Gaytryge made, the singular Poem of Sayne John the Evangelist, the Abbey of the Holy Ghost, etc.; while Mr. Furnivall has added, besides the curious Poems on the Pilgrim's Sea-Voyage and the Parliament of Devils, etc., those tender Hymns to the Virgin and Christ, that simple Prayer of Richard de Castre's, whose pathos all must feel. The issue of the revised version of Hampole's *Office* promised in our last Report has been postponed, as a better MS. of it than the Thornton one has been found.

In our first class, *Romances*, no work has been issued during the past year in the original series ; and this because the Committee gave notice in their last Report that they would consider " the Arthur and other Romances in the Percy Folio as part of the Society's Texts." No less than twelve Romances, or Romance-Poems, being in the Percy Folio, now all in type,—including three Poems at first intended for the Society's second *Gawaine* volume—the Committee felt absolved from the necessity of producing more. But they regret to hear that the subscriptions to the Folio have not covered half the cost of printing it, and they trust that those Members who have not yet taken the book on the favourable terms at which it has been offered to Members of the Society and their friends, will speedily do so.* In the Extra Series, *The Romance of William of Palerne* (or *William and the Werwolf*) will be issued for 1867 in January or February, 1868, re-edited by Mr. Skeat, with the missing portion supplied from the French original by the kind help of Monsieur Michelant, of the Imperial Library of France. The fragment of an alliterative *Romance of Alexander*, assumed to be by the translator of *William of Palerne*, will be issued in the same volume.

Another most important section of the Society's work, the spread of the study of English in schools, and as a recognised

1855, from the Sloane MS. 2593, contain the *x* forms (*xal*, etc.) as well as the Midland (and Northern) *quan*, *quat*, etc. ; and at p. 74 occur the lines—
" Many merveylis God hajt sent,
Of lytenyng and of thunder dent ;
At the frere ca[r]mys hajt it bent,
At *Lynne* toun, it is non nay.
Lytenyng at *Lynne* dede gret harm,
Of tolbothe and of fryre carm . . .

* It will be remembered that in the proposal for printing the Folio, the promoter said, " without the conviction that these Members [of the Early English Text Society] would back me, I would never have entered on the undertaking ; and the ultimate benefit of it will result to their Society."

branch of education,* has during the last year made a splendid advance. Interest and enquiry have been aroused on all sides, and many of the most thoughtful and able teachers have declared in its favour, as is shown by Professor Seeley's *Lecture*, the *Essays on a Liberal Education*, the proximate establishment of *The London Student*, the introduction of regular English teaching into Marlborough College, King's College School, etc. The Committee believe also that the forthcoming Report of the Schools Commission will take the same view. Mr. Morris's *Specimens of Early English* has been adopted as the Text-book for the B.A. degree in the University of London; and to meet the growing want in schools for early text-books, Mr. Morris has issued his *Selections from Chaucer*, and Mr. Skeat's *Pierce the Ploughman's Crede* has been published separately as a

---

* The Society does not of course desire the study of Early English apart from that of modern and middle English, but as the head and crown of the later work. On the English training in the City School, Mr. Abbott says, in a letter to Mr. Furnivall—" My great object is to influence the home-reading of the boys, and direct it to the English classics instead of trash. For this purpose some classical English work (as for example, Milton's 'Comus,' Pope's 'Iliad,' Scott's 'Ivanhoe,' Scott's 'Marmion,' Milton's 'Paradise Lost')—is allotted to each class from September to Christmas. From Christmas to Easter a play of Shakespeare is substituted. In studying such a work as Pope's 'Iliad,' the boys are expected to know the *plot* of the whole book thoroughly, and they are also expected to get up a part of the work with minute attention to details, the parsing, derivation of words, etc. They are also expected to repeat some passages from memory. I wish a boy who leaves at the age of 16 for business, with perhaps few definite ideas derived from Latin authors, to have derived if possible some definite ideas from English authors. A boy who passes through the middle of the school from the age of 13, suppose, to that of 16, would, in the ordinary course of things, read four plays of Shakespeare, and four other standard English works. His reading would be tested by frequent examinations, and he would be taught the difference between careful reading and careless reading. Such a course might engender a desire of more extended reading, a love of good books, a disgust for bad ones. All this seems to me very valuable. If all boys had good libraries and good homes we might, perhaps, dispense with a part of our English training (though even then a boy could not derive all the benefit from home-reading that he could from home-reading tested by school-examination), but, as things are, I consider our English training indispensable.

"Here are some of the books studied in different classes—beginning from the lowest in the senior school:—

Grammar Class.	(*By heart*)	{ "Ruin seize thee."	......	Gray.
		{ "Ivanhoe."	......	Scott.
I Class.	(*By heart*)	{ "Ivry."	......	Macaulay.
		{ "Quentin Durward."	...	Scott.
II Class.		"Marmion."	......	Scott.
III Class.	(*By heart*)	{ "Allegro and Penseroso."		Milton.
		{ "Old Mortality."	......	Scott.
Latin Class.		Pope's "Iliad."		
IV Class.		{ "Paradise Lost," (two books).		
		{ Trench on "Words."		
(*For this year,* 1867.) V Class.		{ A book of the "Faery Queen."		
		{ 1st part of Angus' "Handbook."		
(*For this year.*)		{ "Piers Plowman's Crede."		
VI Class.		{ Dante's "Inferno" (Carey).		
		{ Angus' "Handbook."		

school book. Professor Hiram Corson's edition of Chaucer's *Legend of Good Women* is also here worthy of note. The foundation of an Anglo-Saxon professorship at Cambridge by a member of the Society, the Rev. Professor Bosworth, has been announced, and when completed will rescue that seat of learning from the disgrace it has hitherto laboured under, that the University of Spenser, Ben Jonson, Bacon, Milton, Wordsworth, Byron, Macaulay, and Tennyson, has had no recognised teacher of their mother tongue. Well has Professor Seeley said,* "Classical studies may make a man intellectual, but the study of the native literature has a moral effect as well. *It is the true ground and foundation of patriotism.* . . We too are a great historic nation; we too have 'titles manifold.' This country is not some newly discovered island in the Northern seas. . . . . But the name of Milton sounds like any other name to those who have not pondered over his verses. I call that man uncivilized who is not connected with the past through the state in which he lives, and sympathy with the great men who have lived in it." Whencesoever the mighty of old come, we can set their peers beside any, their lords over many, from the rolls of our early and middle times, and in the knowledge of these men's words and thoughts lies one of the springs of the regeneration of our land.

In connection with the study of Early English, the Committee allude also with special gratification to its spread in Germany; to the completion of Dr. Stratmann's 'Dictionary of the Old English Language, compiled from Writings of the XIII, XIV and XV centuries,'—the best book of its kind;—the same editor's announced edition of the *Owl and Nightingale* from the MSS.; and the appearance of Mätzner and Goldbeck's *Sprachproben*, or 'Specimens of Early English,' which though unluckily not re-edited from the MSS., contains elaborate notes and careful Introductions that reflect the highest credit on the editors.

The winners of the Society's Prizes in 1867 for the study of English before Chaucer were:—

Winners.	Examiners.†
Alexander Monro.	
George Lever Widemann. }	Rev. Prof. Bosworth, Oxford.
John Bradshaw.	Prof. Dowden, Trinity Coll., Dublin
Henry A. Harben.	„ Morley, Univ. Coll., London.
	„ Brewer, King's Coll., London.
Boswell Berry	„ Masson, Edinburgh.
W. Taylor Smith.	„ A. W. Ward, Owen's Coll., Manchester.
Laurence Thomson.	„ Nichol, Glasgow.
George Crighton.	„ Baynes, St. Andrew's.
W. G. Rushbrooke.	Rev. E. A. Abbott, City of London School.

* Macmillan's Magazine, November, 1867, p. 86, Lecture on *English in Schools*.
† From a misunderstanding, Professor Moffatt, of Galway, did not examine for the Society's prize. The pupils of Prof. Rushton, of Cork, were absent at the Civil Service Examinations when the College ones were held.

The Committee have again to return thanks to the several Professors and Mr. Abbott, for the trouble they have taken in giving lectures and holding examinations for these prizes. It is gratifying to know that in one instance at least, the Society's prize has induced the best man of his year at a college to take up the study of Early English, and so to gain a possession above the worth of mere prizes.

The result of the past year's work is such as to call on every Member for increased exertion to extend the sphere of the Society's usefulness and operations. It is hindered on every side by want of funds, by want of attention from men in the hurry of business or fashionable life; and in securing either or both of these, Members will do good service to their Society.

For this new year of 1868, the Committee will issue to Members with this Report:—1. The very interesting set of Instructions to Parish Priests, by John Mirk, Canon of Lilleshall, in Shropshire, edited for the first time, from the best MS., by Mr. Edward Peacock. Its sketch of the life and duties both of priest and layman, is full of life-like touches and curious information. 2. In contrast with this, the even more curious and full picture of the outer life of page and duke, of school-boy and girl, of olden time, contained in the largest collection of verse treatises yet made on the Manners and Meals of our ancestors, edited by Mr. Furnivall, entitled *The Babees Book, etc.*, and having Forewords on Education in Early England before 1450 A.D. 3. Another most curious Treatise on Female Education in the fourteenth century,—*The Knight de la Tour Landry*, edited by Mr. Thomas Wright,—showing how then, by precept and the citation of examples, a father taught his motherless girls to "learn and see both the good and evil of the time past, and for to keep them in good cleanness, and from all evil in time coming."* To these the Committee propose to add:—4. Perhaps the most important linguistic text issued by the Society, *Early English Homilies*, ab. 1200 A.D., edited by Mr. Richard Morris, showing a stage in the development of English Noun-inflexions, hitherto unknown and unexpected, and exhibiting an extraordinary confusion of forms, besides most pleasant quaintnesses of speech, of thought, and life. 5. The Third Part of the Romance of *Merlin*, edited by Mr. H. B. Wheatley. 6. Part III. of Sir David Lyndesay's Works, *The Historie and Testament of Squyer Meldrum*, edited by Dr. F. Hall. And the Committee trust that Members will supply funds enough to enable the *Gawaine*

* Immediate payment of the present year's subscriptions is required, in order that the printers' bills for these Texts may be discharged; and the Committee again request each Member to direct his Banker to pay his Subscription on every 1st of January to the Society's account, at the Regent-street Branch of the Union Bank.

Poems, the short Anglo-Saxon *Finding of the Holy Cross*, the *Alliterative Romance of the Destruction of Troy*, Text B. of *Langland's Vision of Piers Plowman*, and the *Catholicon*, to be included in this year's issue, for the books can be ready whenever the money for them is forthcoming.

For the EXTRA SERIES the year's issue will be:—

1. Caxton's Book of Curtesye, in Three Versions:—1, from the unique printed copy in the Cambridge University Library; 2, from the Oriel MS. 79; 3, from the Balliol MS. 354. Edited by F. J. Furnivall, Esq., M.A.
[*To be issued with " William of Palerne."*
2. Havelok the Dane. Re-edited from the unique MS. by the Rev. W. W. Skeat, M.A., with the sanction and aid of the original editor, Sir Frederic Madden.
3. Chaucer's Prose Works. Part II. Edited from the MSS. by Richard Morris, Esq.

The Committee desire to express their warm thanks to Sir Frederic Madden for withdrawing his formerly expressed wish that *Havelok* should not be re-edited by the Society, and for now nominating Mr. Skeat to reproduce in a more accessible form, the Text so much desired by Students,—a Text whose reputation is so largely due to the great ability and care of him who first gave it to the small public of the Roxburghe Club.

With regard to the large-paper copies of the Extra Series, the Committee give notice that when the number of pages issued becomes so large as to leave little or no profit to the Society, the subscription to the large-paper copies will be raised. The cost of the hand-made laid paper for these is very heavy, fifty-four shillings a ream, and though the subscribers will probably get for two guineas double the quantity of matter that, and on better paper than, the Roxburghe Club members get for five guineas, yet when the year's issue exceeds two moderate, or three thin volumes, it can be produced only at a loss of the profit that these large-papers are expected to yield. And as the Society has from the first set its face against luxurious editions except as a help to working ones, the large-papers must fulfil the condition of yielding that help, or the Society cannot consent to produce them.

The REPRINTING FUND has now 90 Subscribers, and their subscriptions, with £47 from the sale of back Texts, will enable the Texts of 1864 to go to press at once, and there can be no doubt that this year will see them all reprinted.

The Committee invite offers of voluntary assistance from those who may be willing to edit or copy Texts, or to lend them books for reprinting or for re-reading with the original MSS.

The Subscription to the Society is £1 1s. a year [and £1 1s. (Large Paper £2 2s.) additional for the EXTRA SERIES], due in advance on the 1st of JANUARY, and should be paid either to the Society's Account at the Union Bank of London, 14, Argyll Place, Regent Street, W., or by post-office order (made payable to the Chief Office, London) to the Hon. Secretary, HENRY B. WHEATLEY, Esq., 53, Berners Street, London, W.

List of Texts for Publication in future years:

I. ARTHUR AND OTHER ROMANCES.

The Alliterative Romance of the Destruction of Troy, translated from Guido de Colonna. To be edited from the unique MS. in the Hunterian Museum, Glasgow, by the Rev. G. A. Panton, and D. Donaldson, Esq. *[In the Press.*
Merlin, Part IV. To be edited by H. B. Wheatley, Esq. *[Copied.*
The Romance of Arthour and Merlin. Re-edited* from the Auchinleck MS. (ab. 1320-30 A.D), and the Lincoln's Inn and Douce MSS.
The History of the Saint Graal or Sauk Ryal. By Henry Lonelich Skynner, (ab. 1440 A.D.) To be re-edited from the unique MS. in the Library of Corpus Christi Coll., Cambridge, by F. J. Furnivall, Esq., M.A.
Le Morte Arthur, re-edited from the Harl. MS. 2252, by F. J. Furnivall, Esq., M.A.
The Arthur Ballads.
The Romance of Sir Tristrem. To be re-edited from the Auchinleck MS.
The Romance of Sir Generides in Ballad Metre, from the unique MS. in Trin. Coll., Library, Cambridge. To be edited by W. Aldis Wright, Esq., M.A.
The English Charlemagne Romances, re-edited from the Auchinleck MS., Lansd. 381, etc.
Sir Ferumbras, a Charlemagne Romance in Southern verse (ab. 1377 A.D.): from MS. Ashmole 33. *[Part copied.*
The Romance or Legend of Sir Ypotis. From the Vernon and other MSS. *[Copied.*
The English Alexander Romances. Chevelere Assigne.
The Early English Version of the Gesta Romanorum. To be re-edited from the MSS. in the British Museum and other Libraries.

II. DIALECTAL WORKS AND DICTIONARIES.

The Gospel of Nicodemus in the Northumbrian dialect. To be edited for the first time from Harl. MS. 4196, etc., Cotton-Galba, E. ix., by R. Morris, Esq.
[Part copied.
Lives of Saints, in the Southern dialect. To be edited from the Harleian MS. 2277 (ab. 1305 A.D.) by R. Morris, Esq.
Barbour's Lives of Saints (in the Northern dialect). From the MS. in the Cambridge University Library.
Audelay's Works in the Shropshire Dialect. To be edited from the Douce MS. 302, by Richard Morris, Esq. *[Part copied.*

A Series of Early-English Dictionaries.

Catholicon Anglicum. An English-Latin Dictionary (A.D. 1480). To be edited from Lord Monson's MS. by H. B. Wheatley, Esq. *[Copied.*
A little Dictionary for Children (W. de Worde), or a shorte Dictionarie for yonge beginners (1554), by J. Withals. (The earliest edition, to be collated with the succeeding editions.) To be edited by Joseph Payne, Esq.
Abcedarium Anglico-latinum, pro Tyrunculis, Richardo Huloeto exscriptore. Londini, 1552. To be edited by Danby P. Fry, Esq.
An Alvearie, or Quadruple Dictionarie in Englishe, Latin, Greeke, and French, by John Baret. (The edition of 1580 collated with that of 1573.)

Also, Latin-English,—

Horman's Vulgaria, 1519, 1530. To be edited by Toulmin Smith, Esq.

---

* The re-editions may, and probably will, be transferred to the *Extra Series*, as the getting out of the different works must depend on the power and convenience of the Editors who devote their time and energies to the Society's service, and on the relative amounts subscribed to the Original and Extra Series. The income of each Series should be raised to a thousand a year. The present lists contain probably £20,000 worth of work. Another £40,000 to that would perhaps finish the Society's task; and with a will the work may be done by the present generation. We have now fair hold of it, and should resolve not to loosen our hold till all the work is down.

III. MISCELLANEOUS.

The two later and differing Versions of Langland's Vision of Piers Plowman, Texts B and C, in separate editions, with a volume of Notes, Glossary, etc. To be edited from the MSS. by the Rev. W. W. Skeat, M.A. [*Preparing.*

Chaucer. The Household Accounts of Elizabeth, wife of Prince Lionel, in which Chaucer is mentioned; with the other Documents relating to the Poet. To be edited by E. A. Bond, Esq., Keeper of the MSS. in the British Museum.

Mayster Jon Gardener, and other early pieces on Herbs, etc. To be edited from the MSS. by W. Aldis Wright, Esq., M.A. [*Copied.*

Early English Treatises on Music—Descant, the Gamme, etc.—from MSS. in London and Oxford. To be edited by the Rev. W. M. Snell, M.A., Fellow of Corpus Christi Coll., Cambridge. [*Part copied.*

Carols and Songs, Religious and Secular, chiefly from inedited MSS. To be edited by F. J. Furnivall, Esq., M.A. [*Copied.*

Early English Poems from the Vernon MS. To be edited by F. J. Furnivall, Esq., M.A. [*Part copied.*

Palladius on Husbondrie; the earliest English Poem on Husbandry. To be edited from the unique MS. in Colchester Castle (ab. 1425 A.D.) by the Rev. Barton Lodge, A.M. Part I. [*In the Press.*

Sir David Lyndesay's Works, Part IV. To be edited by F. Hall, Esq., D.C.L.

The Rewle of the Moon, and other Poems illustrating Superstitions. To be edited from MSS. by F. J. Furnivall, Esq., M.A. [*Part copied.*

Vegecius of Knyghthod and Chyualrie, from MSS. in the Bodleian and British Museum. To be edited by Danby P. Fry, Esq. [*Copied.*

The Siege of Rouen. From Harl. MS. 2256, Egerton MS. 1995, Harl. 753, Bodl. 3562 (E. Musæs 124), etc.

Lydgate's Tragedies of Bochas, or Falles of Princes. From the fine Harleian MS. 1766.

Lydgate and Burgh's Secreta Secretorum. From the Sloane MS. 2464.

The Story of Two Merchants, from the Cambridge Univ. MS. IIh. iv. 12, (ab. 1450, A.D.), with a tale from the Porkington MS., No. 10.

Lydgate's Translation of Boethius, A.D. 1410; Pilgrim, 1426; Siege of Thebes, 1448–50, and other Poems.

Hugh Campden's Sidracke. From MS. Laud, G. 57; Harl. 4294, etc.

Occleve's Unprinted Works.

Occleve's De Regimine Principum, re-edited from Arundel MS. 38.

Le Venery de Twety and of Mayster John Giffarde, and the Mayster of Game. From MSS. Cott. Vesp. B xii., Harl. 5806, etc. To be edited by Alfred Sadler, Esq.

An Old English Bestiary of ab. 1250 A.D. To be edited from an Arundel MS. by R. Morris, Esq. [*Copied.*

Cato, Great and Little, with Proverbs, etc., from the Vernon and other MS. To be edited by Mr. Edmund Brock. [*Copied.*

Gawain Douglas's Æneis. To be edited by F. Hall, Esq., D.C.L.

Barbour's Troy-Book. The Fragments in the MSS. of the Cambridge University Library, and the Douce Collection.

The Siege of Jerusalem, two Texts: 1. from a Cambridge Univ. MS., Cot. Calig. A. ii., etc.; 2. from an Oxford Univ. MS., and Calig. A. ii. To be edited by the Rev. J. R. Lumby, M.A.

The Nightingale, and other Poems, from MS. Cot. Addit. MS. 10,036, etc.

Lauder's remaining Poems. To be edited by F. Hall, Esq., D.C.L.

Early Lawes and Ordinances of Warre. To be edited by the Rev. T. F. Simmons.

George Ashby's Active Policy of a Prince, from MS. MM. iv. 42, in Cam. Univ. Library.

Peter Idle's Poems, from the MS. EE. iv. 37, in Camb. Univ. Library.

Adam Davie's Poems, from M.S. Laud. 1. 74, and Hale's MS. 150. To be edited by the Rev. J. R. Lumby, M.A.

A Collection of Early Tracts on Grammar. To be edited (chiefly from MSS. for the first time) by H. B. Wheatley, Esq. [*Part copied.*

Municipal Records of England. To be edited from MSS. by Toulmin Smith, Esq.

Some of Francis Thynne's Works. To be edited from the MSS. by G. H. Kingsley, Esq., M.D.

Skelton's Translation of Diodorus Siculus, oute of freshe Latin, that is, of Poggius Florentinus, containing six books. To be edited for the first time from the unique MS. in the Library of Corpus Christi Coll., Cambridge.

IV. BIBLICAL AND RELIGIOUS.

The Finding of the Holy Cross, from an Anglo-Saxon MS., with an Early English Poem on the Cross. Edited by Richard Morris, Esq. [*In the Press.*

The Life of St. Juliane, in Early English: two Versions from MSS. To be edited by the Rev. J. Oswald Cockayne, M.A. [*In the Press.*

The Rewle of Saint Benet, in Anglo-Saxon, Semi-Saxon, and Early English, also in Northern verse of the 15th century, and prose of the 15th and 16th. Five texts. To be edited from early MSS. and Cotton MS. Vesp. A. xxv. by R. Morris, Esq. [*In the Press.*

Dan Jeremy's Lay-Folks' Mass-Book, and other Poems on the Mass. To be edited from a Royal MS., etc., by the Rev. T. F. Simmons. [*Part copied.*

Life of St. Katherine, and other early pieces before 1250 A.D. To be edited from the MSS. (with a translation) by the Rev. Oswald Cockayne, M.A. [*Copied.*

Early English Homilies ab. 1220-30 A.D. To be edited from the unique MS. in the Library of Trinity College, Cambridge, by R. Morris, Esq. [*Copied.*

Cursor Mundi, or Cursur o Worlde, in the Northern Dialect. To be edited from the MSS. in the British Museum and Trinity College, Cambridge, by Richard Morris, Esq. Part I. [*Copied.*

The Psalms called Schorham's. To be edited from the unique MS. (ab. 1340 A.D.) in the British Museum, by R. Morris, Esq. [*Copied.*

Roberd of Brunne's Handlyng Synne; a treatise on the sins, and sketches of the manners of English men and women in A.D. 1303. To be re-edited from the MSS. in the British Museum and Bodleian Libraries, by F. J. Furnivall, Esq., M.A.

The Harrowing of Hell. To be edited from MSS., in the Bodleian Library, etc., by R. F. Weymouth, Esq., M.A. [*Copied.*

Hampole's Translation of, and Commentary on, the Psalms, from the Northern MSS. in Sidney Sussex Coll., Cambridge, and No. 10 in Eton College Library, etc. To be edited by R. Morris, Esq. [*Part copied.*

Hampole's remaining Works.

þe Clowde of Unknowyng, from MS. Harl. 2373.

A Lanterne of Lit), from Harl. MS. 2324.

Early English Directions for the Confessional, from Sloane and other MSS.

The Old and New Testament in Verse. To be edited from the Vernon MS. by R. Morris, Esq. [*Copied.*

The Stories of Lazarus, Susanna and the Elders, etc. From the Vernon MS. To be edited by J. W. Hales, Esq., M.A. [*Copied.*

The History of Adam and Eve. From the Vernon MS. Harl. 1704, etc. Edited by S. W. Kershaw, Esq. [*Copied.*

Amon and Mardocheus, or Haman and Mordecai. From the Vernon MS.

Trevisa's Translation of Fitzralf's Sermon. From MS. Harl. 1900.

Medytacions of the Soper of our Lorde Ihesu, etc., perhaps by Robert of Brunne. To be edited from the Harl. MS. 1701 (ab. 1360 A.D.), etc., by F. J. Furnivall, Esq.

Guillaume de Deguilleville's Pilgrimage of the Sowle, translated. From MS. Cott. Vitel. c. xiii.

Lydgate's Life of St. Edmund. From the presentation MS. to Henry VI. Harl. 2278

William of Nassyngton's Treatise on Sins, etc.

John de Taysteke's Poem on the Decalogue, 1357 A.D. From MS. Harl. 1022.

EXTRA SERIES (OF RE-EDITIONS).

Chaucer's Prose Works. Parts III. and IV.

Syr Thomas Maleore's Kynge Arthur, from Caxton's edition of 1485. [*Ready for Press.*

Barbour's Brus, from the MS. in St. John's Coll., Cambridge, etc., to be edited by J. Peile, Esq., M.A., and the Rev. W. W. Skeat, M.A. [*Preparing.*

Harrison's Description of England. Part II. From Holinshed's Chronicle.

The Complaynte of Scotland, 1548. Blind Harry's Wallace, from the MS.

The Voiage and Travaile of Sir John Maundeville, Knight, written A.D. 1356; from the Cotton MS. Titus C xvi., etc. To be edited by Richard Morris. Esq.
Trevisa's Translation of Bartholomew Glanville de Proprietatibus Rerum.
Froissart's Chronicles, translated out of Frenche into our maternal Englyshe Tonge, by Johan Bourchier, Knight, Lord Berners. To be edited by Henry B. Wheatley, Esq. (if not reprinted in *English Reprints*.)
Lord Berners's Translation of Thystory of Arthur of Lytle Brytayne.
Ancient Mysteries, from the Digby MS.
The Wyse Chylde of Thre Yere Olde (W. de Worde); with the Civilitie of Childehode, translated by T. Paynell, 1560, and other early Treatises on Education. To be edited by F. J. Furnivall, Esq., M.A.
John Hart's Orthographie, 1569, and Methode to read English, 1570.
Bullokar's Booke at large for the Amendment of Orthography, 1580, 1586.
Mulcaster's Positions 1561, and Elementarie, 1582.
W. Bullokar's Orthographie, 1580, and Bref Grammar, 1586.
Brinsley's Ludus Literarius, or the Grammar Schoole, 1627.
Sir Thomas Elyot's Governor, and other works.
Juliana Berners' Bokys of Hawkyng and Huntyng, and also of Cootarmuris, 1486, with the Treatyse of Fysshynge with an Angle, 1496.
Caxton's Curial made by Mayster Alain Charretier (1484-5).
———— Book of Good Maners, 1487.
———— Fayt of Armes and of Chyualrye, from Christine of Pisa (1489).
The Forme of Cury. Coryat's Crambe, 1611. Coryat's Crudities, 1611.
Andrew Boorde's Compendyous Regyment, or a Dyetary of Helth (ab. 1542).
Andrew Borde's Introduction of Knowledge.
Bulleyn's Bulwarke of Defence or the Booke of Simples.
The English Works of Sir Thomas More. Scotish Poems before 1600 A.D.
A Myrrovre for Magistrates. A Volume of Moralities. A Volume of Interludes.
Stubbes's Anatomie of Abuses. The Northumberland Household Book.
Puttenham's Arte of English Poesie. Fitzherbert's Husbandry.

*** *All Complaints as to the Non-delivery of Texts should be made to the Publisher.*

The Publications for 1864 are:
1. Early English Alliterative Poems, ab. 1320-30 A.D., ed. R. Morris.
2. Arthur, ab. 1440, ed. F. J. Furnivall.
3. Lauder on the Dewtie of Kyngis, etc., 1556, ed. F. Hall.
4. Sir Gawayne and the Green Knight, ab. 1320-30, ed. R. Morris.

The Publications for 1865 are:—
5. Hume's Orthographie and Congruitie of the Britan Tongue, ab. 1617, ed. H. B. Wheatley.
6. Lancelot of the Laik, ab. 1500, ed. Rev. W. W. Skeat.
7. Genesis and Exodus, ab. 1250, ed. R. Morris.
8. Morte Arthure, ab. 1440, ed. Rev. G. G. Perry.
9. Thynne on Chaucer's Works, ab. 1598, ed. Dr. Kingsley.
10. Merlin, ab. 1450, Part I., ed. H. B. Wheatley.
11. Lyndesay's Monarche, etc., 1552, Part I., ed. F. Hall.
12. The Wright's Chaste Wife, ab. 1462, ed. F. J. Furnivall.

The Publications for 1866 are:—
13. Seinte Marherete, 1200-1330, ed. Rev. O. Cockayne.
14. King Horn, Floris and Blancheflour, etc., ed. Rev. J. R. Lumby.
15. Political, Religious, and Love Poems, ed. F. J. Furnivall.
16. The Book of Quinte Essence, ab. 1460-70, ed. F. J. Furnivall.
17. Parallel Extracts from 29 MSS. of Piers Plowman, ed. Rev. W. W. Skeat.
18. Hali Meidenhad, ab. 1200, ed. Rev. O. Cockayne.
19. Lindesay's Monarche, etc., Part II. ed. F. Hall.
20. Hampole's English Prose Treatises, ed. Rev. G. G. Perry.
21. Merlin, Part II. ed. H. B. Wheatley.
22. Partenay or Lusignen, ed. Rev. W. W. Skeat.
23. Dan Michel's Ayenbite of Inwyt, 1340, ed. R. Morris.

The Publications for 1867 are:—
24. Hymns to the Virgin and Christ; the Parliament of Devils, etc., ab. 1430, ed. F. J. Furnivall. 3s.
25. The Stacions of Rome, the Pilgrim's Sea-Voyage, etc., ed. F. J. Furnivall. 2s.
26. Religious Pieces in Prose and Verse, ab. 1440 A.D., ed. Rev. G. G. Perry. 2s.
27. Levins's Manipulus Vocabulorum, 1570, ed. H. B. Wheatley. 12s.
28. Langlands' Vision of Piers Plowman, 1362, A.D. The earliest or Vernon Text, ed. Rev. W. W. Skeat. 7s.
29. English Gilds, their Statutes and Customs, 1389 A.D., ed. Toulmin Smith. 7s.
30. Pierce the Ploughman's Crede, ed. Rev. W. W. Skeat. 2s.

LIST OF SUBSCRIBERS.

COMMITTEE OF MANAGEMENT.

DANBY P. FRY, ESQ.
FREDERICK J. FURNIVALL, ESQ.
FITZEDWARD HALL, ESQ.
REV. J. RAWSON LUMBY.
RICHARD MORRIS, ESQ.
H. T. PARKER, ESQ.

EDWARD PEACOCK, ESQ.
REV. GEORGE G. PERRY.
REV. WALTER W. SKEAT.
TOULMIN SMITH, ESQ.
HENRY B. WHEATLEY, ESQ.
THOMAS WRIGHT, ESQ.

(*With power to add Workers to their number.*)

HONORARY SECRETARY:
HENRY B. WHEATLEY, ESQ., 53, BERNERS STREET, LONDON, W.

BANKERS:
THE UNION BANK OF LONDON, REGENT STREET BRANCH,
14, ARGYLL PLACE, W.

˖ *A star or dagger is prefixed to the names of those who subscribe to the* Extra Series; *a star for the small paper, and a dagger for the large paper.*

ABRAHALL, Rev. John Hoskyns, Combe, near Woodstock.
*ADAM, A. Mercer, Esq., M.D., Boston, Lincolnshire.
ADAM, John, Esq., Town Chamberlain, Greenock.
ADAMS, Dr. Ernest, Anson Road, Victoria Park, Manchester.
*ADAMS, C. E., Esq. (Rouge Dragon), Heralds' College, E.C.
*ADDIS, John, Jun., Esq., Rustington, Littlehampton, Sussex.
AINSWORTH, Dr. R. F., Cliff Point, Lower Broughton, Manchester.
AKROYD, Edward, Esq., Bank Field, Halifax.
ALEXANDER, George Russell, Esq., Glasgow.
†ALEXANDER, John, Esq., Menstriebank, Dowanhill Gardens, Glasgow.
ALEXANDER, Walter, Esq., 29, St. Vincent Street, Glasgow.
ALLON, Rev. Henry, 10, St. Mary's Road, Canonbury, N.
AMERY, J. Sparke, Jun., Esq., Druid, near Ashburton, Devon.
AMHURST, Wm. A. Tyssen, Esq., Didlington Park, Brandon, Norfolk.
ANGUS, Rev. Joseph, D.D., Regent's Park College, N.W.
ARMSTRONG, Hugh Clayton, Esq., Newcastle-on-Tyne.
*ASHER & Co., Messrs., 13, Bedford Street, Covent Garden, W.C. (4 sets).
    Extra Series, 7 sets.
ATHENÆUM CLUB, Waterloo Place, S.W.
ATKINSON, Rev. E., D.D., Master of Clare College, Cambridge.
*ATKINSON, Rev. J. C., Danby Parsonage, Yarm, Yorkshire.
*AUSTIN, Frederick Stephen, Esq., 39, Princess Street, Manchester.
AUSTIN, Stephen, Hertford.

BABINGTON, Rev. Professor Churchill, B.D., St. John's College, Cambridge.
†BACKHOUSE, John H., Esq., Blackwell, Darlington.
†BAIN, J., Esq., 1, Haymarket. *Extra Series*, 1 large and 1 small.
†BAKER, Charles, Esq., 11, Sackville Street, W.
BALTIMORE MERCANTILE LIBRARY.
*BANKS, W. S., Esq., Wakefield.
BARON, Rev. J., Rectory, Upton Scudamore, Warminster, Wilts.
BARRETT, Rev. Alfred, D.D., Carshalton House, Surrey.
†BATY, Rev. Thomas J., Worlabye House, Roehampton, S.W.
BAVERSTOCK, Edwin H., Esq., East Sheen Lodge, Mortlake, Surrey.
BAYNES, Prof. Thos. S., 19, Queen Street, St. Andrew's, Fife.
BEARD, James, Esq., The Grange, Burnage Lane, near Manchester.
BELFAST, THE LIBRARY OF QUEEN'S COLLEGE.
BELL, Rev. W. R., Laithkirk Parsonage, Mickleton, near Barnard Castle.
BENECKE, Dr., Berlin.
BENTLY, Rev. T. R., M.A., St. Matthew's Rectory, Manchester.
BESLY, Rev. Dr. John, The Vicarage, Long Benton, Newcastle-on-Tyne.
BEST, W., Esq., 18, Lyddon Terrace, Leeds.
BICKERTON, G., Esq., 41, Dick Place, Edinburgh.
BIDDELL, Sidney, Esq., Farm-hill House, Stroud, Gloucestershire.
BIGG, Rev. C., The College, Cheltenham.
*BIRMINGHAM LIBRARY, Union Street, Birmingham.
*BIRMINGHAM FREE CENTRAL LIBRARY, Ratcliff Place, Birmingham.
BLACKLEY, Rev. W. L., North Waltham Rectory, Micheldever, Hants.
*BLACKMAN, Frederick, Esq., 4, York Road, S.
*BLADON, James, Esq., Albion House, Pont y Pool.
BOHN, Henry G., Esq., North End House, Twickenham.
BOILEAU, Sir John P., Bart., 20, Upper Brook Street, W.
*BOSWORTH, Rev. Professor, D.D., 20, Beaumont Street, Oxford.
BRIDGMAN, W. D. J., Esq., D.C.L., 11, Victoria Road, Old Charlton, S.E.
BRITTON, John James, Esq., 5, Park Road, Newcastle-on-Tyne.
BROTHERS, Alfred, Esq., 14, St. Ann's Square, Manchester.
*BUCHANAN, Dr. Robert, Prince's Street, Greenock.
BUCKLEY, Rev. Wm. Edw., Rectory, Middleton Cheney, Banbury.
BUMPUS, Mr., 6, Holborn Bars.
*BURRA, James S., Esq., Ashford, Kent.
BUTE, the Marquis of, Christ Church College, Oxford.
BUXTON, Charles, Esq., M.P., 7, Grosvenor Crescent, S.W.

*CAMBRIDGE, CHRIST'S COLLEGE.
*   ,,   TRINITY COLLEGE LIBRARY.
*   ,,   TRINITY HALL LIBRARY.
*CAPARN, Rev. W. B., The Parsonage, Draycot, Weston super Mare.
CAPE TOWN, South African Library, Cape of Good Hope.
CARLYLE, Dr., The Hill, Dumfries, N.B.
CHALMERS, James, Esq., Aberdeen.
*CHALMERS, Richard, Esq., 1, Claremont Terrace, Glasgow.
*CHAMBERLAIN, Arthur, Esq., Moor Green Hall, Moseley, near Birmingham.
*CHAMBERLAIN, Professor John Henry, Christchurch Buildings, Birmingham.
CHAPPELL, William, Esq., Sunninghill, Staines.
CHEETHAM, Rev. S., King's College, London, W.C.
CHELTENHAM COLLEGE LIBRARY.
     ,,   PERMANENT LIBRARY, 18, Clarence Street, Cheltenham.
CHESTERTON, Miss E., 12, Kensington Palace Gardens, W.
CINCINNATI PUBLIC AND SCHOOL LIBRARY.
CLARK, E. C., Esq., Trinity College, Cambridge.

CLARK, Rev. Samuel, The Vicarage, Bredwardine, Hereford.
COHEN, Arthur, Esq., 6, King's Bench Walk, Temple, E.C.
*COLBORNE, William Henry, M.D., Chippenham.
COLEBROOKE, Sir T. Edward, Bart., 37, South Street, Piccadilly.
†COLERIDGE, J. Duke, Esq., Q.C., 6, Southwick Crescent.
COMBE, Thomas, Esq., University Press, Oxford.
*COMPTON, Rev. Lord Alwyne, Chadstone, Northamptonshire.
CONSTABLE, Archibald, Esq., 11, Thistle Street, Edinburgh.
COOPER, John, Esq., 175, Adelaide Road, N.W.
†COSENS, Frederick, Esq., Larkbere Lodge, Clapham Park.
*COWPER, Joseph Meadows, Esq., Davington, Faversham.
COX, Rev. Thomas, The Heath, near Halifax.
*COXHEAD, Albert C., Esq., 47, Russell Square, W.C.
CRAIG, Rev. J. K., Dilamgerbendi Insula, near Ringwood.
CRAIG, Rev. John S., Maryport, Cumberland.
CREAK, A. Esq., The Wick, Brighton.
CREWDSON, Thos. Dilworth, Esq., 8, Cecil Street, Greenheys, Manchester.
CROSSLEY, James, Esq., Booth Street, Piccadilly, Manchester.
CROSTON, James, Esq., Waterloo Road, Cheetham, Manchester.
CROUCH, Walter, jun., Esq., 20, Coborn Street, Bow.
CROWTHER, Joseph S., Esq., 28, Brazennose Street, Manchester.
CULLEY, M. T., Esq., Coupland Castle, Wooler, Northumberland.

DALTON, J. N., Esq., 6, Green Street, Cambridge.
DANA, C. S., Esq., United States.
DARBISHIRE, R. D., Esq., 26, George Street, Manchester.
†DAVIES, Rev. John, Walsoken Rectory, near Wisbeach.
DAVIES, Robert, Esq., The Mount, York.
*DAVIES, W. Carey, Esq., care of Messrs. Grindlay & Co., 55, Parliament Street, S.W.
DAVIS, Henry, Esq., 133, Richmond Road.
DEIGHTON, BELL, & Co., Messrs., Cambridge.
DE LA RUE, Warren, Esq., 110, Bunhill Row, E.C.
DE LA RUE, Wm. Frederick, Esq., 110, Bunhill Row, E.C.
DENTON, Rev. W., 48, Finsbury Circus, E.C.
DEVONSHIRE, The Duke of, Devonshire House, Piccadilly.
DICKINSON, F. H., Esq., Kingweston House, Somerton, Somerset.
*DODDS, Rev. James, The Abbey, Paisley, N.B.
*DONALDSON, David, Esq., Grammar School, Paisley.
DONALDSON, Rev. John, Edinburgh.
D'ORSEY, Rev. A. J., B.D., 9, Upper Seymour Street West, Hyde Park, W.
DOWDEN, Edward, Esq., 61, Wellington Road, Dublin.
DOWSON, Alfred C., Esq., High Dock, Limehouse, E.
DRAKE, W. H., Esq., 2, Newton Terrace, Faversham.
DREW, Alfred, Esq., 2, Raymond Buildings, Gray's Inn, W.C.
DUBLIN, KING'S INN LIBRARY, Henrietta Street.
*   „   Right Rev. Richard C. Trench, Archbishop of Dublin.
DULLEY, Rev. Morton, Barnby Rectory, near Beccles, Suffolk.
DURIEN, W. M., Esq., St. John's College, Cambridge.
DYKES, Frederick, Esq., Wakefield.

*EARLE, Rev. J. Swanswick Rectory, Bath.
EASTWICK, Edward B., Esq., 38, Thurloe Square, S.W.
EDINBURGH UNIVERSITY LIBRARY.
EGGINTON, John, Esq. 13, Friar Street, Reading.
EISDELL, Miss S. L., Colchester.

*ELLIS, A. J., Esq., 25, Argyll Road, Kensington, W.
ELT, C. H., Esq., 1, Noel Street, Islington.
*ELY CATHEDRAL LIBRARY.
†EUING, William, Esq., 209, West George Street, Glasgow.
*EVANS, Sebastian, Esq., 145, Highgate, near Birmingham.
EYTON, J. Walter K., Esq., 46, Portsdown Road, Maida Hill, W.

FAIRBAIRN, Rev. James, Newhaven, near Edinburgh.
*FALCONER, Thomas, Esq., Usk, Monmouthshire.
FAUNTHORPE, Rev. John P., Vice-Principal, Training College, Battersea.
FERGUS, Dr. 30, Elmbank Street, Glasgow.
FIELD, Hamilton, Esq., Thornton Lodge, Thornton Road, Clapham Park.
FISHWICK, Major, Carr Hill, Rochdale.
FITCH, J. G., Esq., Heworth House, York.
FLETCHER, John Shepherd, Esq., Lever Street, Piccadilly, Manchester.
FOGO, David F. Laurie, Esq., 145, West George Street, Glasgow.
*FORSTER, John, Esq., Palace-gate House, Kensington, W.
FOSTER, Ebenezer, Esq., The Elms, Cambridge.
FOWLER, James, Esq., South Parade, Wakefield, Yorkshire.
FRAMES, George C., Esq., 55, Belsize Park, N.W.
*FREEMAN, D. A., Esq., 1, Plowden Buildings, Temple, E.C.
FREETHY, Mr. Frederick, Working Men's College, London.
FROGGATT, Thomas, Esq., Burnage Lane, near Manchester.
FROMMANN, Herr E., Jena.
*FRY, Danby P., Esq., Poor Law Board, Whitehall.
FRY, Frederick Esq., Wellington Street, Islington.
*FURNIVALL, F. J., Esq., 3, Old Square, Lincoln's Inn, W.C.

*GEE, William, Esq., High Street, Boston.
GIBBS, Captain Charles, 2nd Regiment.
GIBBS, H. H., Esq., St. Dunstan's, Regent's Park.
*GIBBS, William, Esq., Tyntesfield, near Bristol, E.
GILBERT, J. T., Esq., Royal Irish Academy, Dublin.
GILLETT, Rev. Edward, Runham Vicarage, Filby, Norwich, *Local Sec.*
GINSBURG, Dr. Chr. D., Brooklea, Aigburth Road, Liverpool.
GIRAUD, Francis F., Esq., South House, Faversham.
GLASGOW UNIVERSITY LIBRARY.
GLEN, W. Cunningham, Esq., Poor Law Board, Whitehall.
GLENNIE, J. Stuart, Esq., 6, Stone Buildings, Lincoln's Inn, W.C.
GODWIN, E. W., Esq., 197, Albany Street, N.W.
GOLDSTÜCKER, Professor, 14, St. George's Square, N.W.
GOLDTHORP, J. D., Esq., Wakefield.
GORDON, Rev. Robert, 14, Northumberland Street, Edinburgh.
GOULBOURN, Rev. Dr., Dean of Norwich, Norwich.
GRAHAME, W. F., Esq., Madras Civil Service.
GREEN, Rev. Henry, Knutsford, Cheshire.
GREG, Louis, Esq., 9, Rumford Street, Liverpool, *Local Sec.*
GREG, Mrs. E. H., Quarry Bank, Wilmslow, Cheshire.
GREY, George, Esq., County Buildings, Glasgow.
GRIFFITH, Rev. H. T., North Walsham, Norfolk.
*GRIFFITH, Robert W., Esq., Quay Street, Cardiff.
GROOME, Rev. R. Monk Soham Rectory, Framlingham Station, Suffolk.
GUEST, Edwin, Esq., LL.D., Master of Caius College, Cambridge.
*GUEST, John. Esq., Moorgate Grange, Rotherham.
*GUILD, J. Wylie, Esq., Glasgow.
*GUILDHALL, LIBRARY OF THE CORPORATION OF LONDON, E.C.

HAILSTONE, E., Esq., Horton Hall, Bradford.
HAINES, Frederick, Esq., 178, Prospect Place, Maida Hill East, W.
HALES, J. W., Esq., Turret Lodge, Park Village East, Regent's Park, N.W.
HALKETT, Samuel, Esq., Advocates' Library, Edinburgh.
HALL, B. H., Esq., Troy, New York.
*HALL, Fitzedward, Esq., D.C.L., 18, Provost Road, Haverstock Hill, N.W.
HALLIWELL, J. O., Esq., 11, Tregunter Road, South Kensington, S.W.
HAMILTON, Andrew, Esq., 47, Rumford Street, Manchester.
HAMLEN, Charles, Esq., 27, Virginia Street, Glasgow.
HANSON, Reginald, Esq., 37, Boundary Road, N.W.
HARBEN, Henry A., Esq., Seaford Lodge, Fellows' Road, N.W.
HARRIS, Frederick, Esq., Liverpool.
HARRIS, Mortimer, Esq., 16, Marlborough Hill, St. John's Wood, N.W.
*HARRIS, William, Esq., Stratford Road, Camp Hill, Birmingham.
HARRISON, Wm., Esq., Samlesbury Hall, near Blackburn, Lancashire.
HART, Howard, Esq., Troy, New York.
HAYES, Francis B., Esq., United States.
HEALES, Alfred, Esq., Doctors' Commons, E.C.
HERFORD, Edward, Esq., The Knolls, Alderley Edge, near Manchester.
HERFORD, Rev. W. H., 33, Wood Street, Greenheys, Manchester.
HEWITT, Thomas, Esq., Bella Vista, Queen's Town, Cork Harbour.
HILL, John William, Esq., 3, Osborne Terrace, Leeds.
HILTON, Wm. Hughes, Esq., Willow Bank, Stretford, near Manchester.
HODGKIN, Mrs., West Derby, Liverpool.
*HODGSON, Shadworth H., Esq., 45, Conduit Street, Regent Street, W.
HOETS, J. W. Van Rees, Esq., 150, Adelaide Road, N.W.
HOOPER, John, Esq., University College, Gower Street, W.C.
HOPKINS, Hugh, Bookseller, 6, Royal Bank Place, Glasgow.
HOPWOOD, J. R., Esq., Trinity College, Cambridge.
HORWOOD, Alfred J., Esq., New Court, Middle Temple, E.C.
†HOUGHTON, Lord, 16, Upper Brook Street, W.
HOWARD, Henry, Esq., Albion Tube Works, Nile Street, Birmingham.
HOWARD, Hon. Richard E., D.C.L., Stamp Office, Manchester.
HUGO, Rev. Thomas, The Chestnuts, Clapton, N.E.
HUTCHINSON, Captain R. R., 13, Holland Terrace, Holland Road, Kensington.
*HYDE, James John, Esq., 10, Lomas Buildings, Bull Lane, Stepney, E.

INDIA OFFICE LIBRARY, St. James's, S.W.
INGLEBY, C. Mansfield, Esq., LL.D., Valentines, Ilford, E.

JACKSON, E. Steane, Esq., Tettenhall Proprietary School, near Wolverhampton.
*JACKSON, John, Esq., Chancery Place, Manchester.
*JACKSON, Rev. S., Magdalen College, Cambridge.
JEFFERY, Counsell, Esq., 30, Tredegar Square, Bow Road, E.
*JENKINS, James, M.D., Royal Marine Infirmary, Plymouth.
JENNER, Charles, Esq., Easter Duddingston Lodge, Edinburgh.
*JESSOPP, Rev. A., The School House, Norwich.
JOHNSON, Prof. G. J., 243, Hagley Road, Edgbaston, Birmingham.
JOHNSON, S. G., Esq., Faversham.
JOHNSON, W., Esq., Eton College, Windsor.
JONES, C. W., Esq., Gateacre, near Liverpool.
*JONES, J. Pryce, Esq., Grove Park School, Wrexham.
*JONES, Joseph, Esq., Abberley Hall, Stourport.
*JONES, Thomas, Esq., Chetham Library, Manchester.

JONES, W. Stavenhagen, Esq., Leadenhall Buildings, 79½, Gracechurch Street, E.C.
*JORDAN, Joseph, Esq., Bridge Street, Manchester.

KENDALL, J., Esq., 97, Rumford Street, Manchester.
KENRICK, William, Esq., Mountlands, Norfolk Road, Birmingham.
KERSHAW, John, Esq., Cross Gate, Audenshaw, Manchester.
*KERSLEY, Rev. Canon, LL.D., Middleton Vicarage, King's Lynn.
KETT, Rev. C. W., 16, Gloucester Road, Regent's Park, N.W.
*KING, W. Warwick, Esq., 29, Queen Street, Cannon Street West, E.C.
KITSON, James, Esq., Elmete Hall, Leeds.
KOCH, Dr. (care of Dr. C. Schaible).

LAIDLAY, A., Esq., 13, Great Stuart Street, Edinburgh, and Queen's College, Oxford.
LAING, David, Esq., LL.D., Signet Library, Edinburgh.
*LANCASHIRE INDEPENDENT COLLEGE, Manchester.
LANCASTER, W. T., Esq., Lower Taufield Street, Caledonian Street, Leeds.
LATHAM, Henry, Esq., 34, Beaumont Street, Oxford.
LAWRENCE, A. C., Esq., *Chronicle* Office, Tavistock Street, Covent Garden.
†LEIGH, John, Esq., Whalley Road, Whalley Range, Manchester, *Local Sec.*
LEEDS OLD LIBRARY.
LEWIS, Henry, Esq., Secretary Training College, Battersea.
LINNELL, J., jun., Esq., Redhill, Reigate.
LITTLE, William, C., Esq., Stag's Holt, March, Cambridgeshire.
*LODGE, Rev. Barton, Colchester.
*LONDON LIBRARY, 12, St. James's Square, S.W.
LUARD, Rev. Henry Richards, 4, St. Peter's Terrace, Cambridge.
LUCK, Frederick George, Esq., West Farm, East Barnet, Herts.
LUDLOW, John, Esq., Whalley Road, Whalley Range, Manchester.
*LUMBY, Rev. J. Rawson, St. Mary's Gate, Cambridge.
LUSHINGTON, E. L., Esq., Park House, Maidstone, and Glasgow.

MACCABE, Mr. John, Bookseller, Wakefield.
*MAC DONALD, George, Esq., The Retreat, Upper Mall, Hammersmith, W.
MAC DOUALL, Professor Charles, LL.D., Queen's College, Belfast.
MACKENZIE, John Whitefoord, Esq., 16, Royal Circus, Edinburgh.
MACKINTOSH, James, Esq., 1, West End Park Street, Woodland Road, Glasgow.
MACLAREN, John Rattray, Esq., Edinburgh.
*M'LAUGHLIN, Captain E., R.A., Radnor Cliff, Sandgate.
MCLENNAN, Rev. A., The Rectory, Sunderland.
MACMILLAN, A., Esq., Bedford Street, Covent Garden, W.C.
†MACMILLAN & Co., Messrs., Cambridge (3 sets). *Extra Series*, 3 copies small and 1 large.
*MADDEN, Sir Frederick, K.H., 25, St. Stephen's Square.
MALLESON, William T., Esq., Henmeadow, Freshwater, Isle of Wight.
MANCHESTER, The Duke of, Kimbolton Castle, St. Neot's.
MANCHESTER, The Lord Bishop of, Mauldreth Hall, near Manchester.
MANCHESTER PORTICO LIBRARY.
MANNING, Miss, 34, Blomfield Road, Maida Hill, W.
MARKBY, Rev. Thomas, Trinity Hall, Cambridge.
MARSH, His Excellency George P., Florence.
*MARTINEAU, P. M., Esq., Littleworth, Esher, Surrey.
*MARTINEAU, Russell, Esq., British Museum, W.C.
*MAYOR, Rev. John E. B., St. John's College, Cambridge.

Medley, Rev. J. B., Tormarton Rectory, Chipping Sodbury.
†Medlicott, W. G., Esq., Longmeadow, Massachusetts, U. S.
*Melbourne Public Library, Victoria.
Melbourne University, Victoria.
Monk, F. W., Esq., Faversham.
Monro, J., Esq., 131, Richmond Road.
Monson, The Lord, Burton Hall, Lincolnshire.
Moreshwar, Mr., 3, St. George's Square, Primrose Hill, N.W.
Morris, Richard, Esq., 10, Stamford Road, Page Green, Tottenham.
Muir, John, Esq., D.C.L., LL.D., 16, Regent's Terrace, Edinburgh.
Müller, Professor Max, Park's End, Oxford.
Munby, Arthur J., Esq., 6, Fig-tree Court, Temple, E.C.
*Muntz, George H. M., Esq., Birchfield, Birmingham.
Murdoch, James Barclay, Esq., 33, Lynedoch Street, Glasgow.

*Napier, George W., Esq., Alderley Edge, near Manchester.
Neaves, Lord, 7, Charlotte Square, Edinburgh.
Neumann, Edward, Esq., 37, Ethelburga House, 70, Bishopsgate Street, E.C.
*Newcastle-upon-Tyne Literary and Philosophical Society.
Nichol, Professor, University, Glasgow.
Nichols, John Gough, Esq., 25, Parliament Street, Westminster.
Noble, Benjamin, Esq., 74, Union Street, Greenock.
Norfolk and Norwich Literary Institution, Norwich.
*Norman, J. Manship, Esq., Dencombe, Crawley, Sussex.
Norris, Edwin, Esq., 6, St. Michael's Grove, Brompton, S.W.
*Norris, William, Esq., 7, St. James's Square, Manchester.
*Norwich Grammar School Library.

*Oakey, John, jun., Esq., 172, Blackfriars Road, S.
Odell, A. J., Esq., New York.
Ogle, Messrs. Maurice & Co., Glasgow.
Oppenheim, Mrs. Chas., 29, Hamilton Terrace, St. John's Wood Road, N.W.
Ormerod, Henry M., Esq., 5, Clarence Street, Manchester.
Oscott, Library of St. Mary's College, Birmingham.
Owen's College Library, Manchester.
*Oxford and Cambridge Club, Pall Mall.

†Paine, Cornelius, Jun., Esq., Oak Hill, Surbiton, Surrey.
Palmer, A. Smythe, Esq., Ashbrook, Raheny, Co. Dublin.
†Panton, Rev. G. A., Crown Circus, Dowanhill, Glasgow, *Local Sec.* (2 sets).
    Extra Series, 1 large and 1 small.
†Parker, H. T., Esq., 3, Ladbroke Gardens, W. (11 sets.) *Extra Series*,
    11 small and 1 large.
Patterson, W. S., Esq., Glasgow.
*Payne, Joseph, Esq., 4, Kildare Gardens, Bayswater, W.
*Peace, Maskell Wm., Esq., Greenhill, Wigan, Lancashire.
Peacock, Edward, Esq., Bottesford Manor, Brigg, Lincolnshire.
Peacock, William, Esq., 3, Sunniside, Sunderland.
Pearson, C. H., Esq., Oriel College, Oxford.
Peel, George, Esq., Soho Iron Works, Manchester.
Peile, John, Esq., Christ's College, Cambridge.
*Penfold, Hugh, Esq., Library Chambers, Middle Temple.
Pennsylvania, Historical Society of, Philadelphia.
Penzance Public Library.
Perceval, Charles Spencer, Esq., 64, Eccleston Square, S.W.
Perry, Rev. George G., Waddington Rectory, Lincoln.

PICTON, James A., Esq., Dale Street, Liverpool.
*POCOCK, Charles Innes, Esq., Rouge Bouillon, Jersey.
PORTSMOUTH ATHENÆUM, Portsmouth, U.S.
POTTS, C. Y., Esq., Ledbury, Herefordshire.
PRANGE, F. G., Esq., 2, Grove Park, Lodge Lane, Liverpool.
*PRIAULX, Osw. De Beauvoir, Esq., 8, Cavendish Square, W.
PRITCHARD, James, Esq., Lendel Place, Paisley Road.
PROVAN, Moses, Esq., 110, West George Street, Glasgow.
PUTNAM, G. Phelps, Esq., United States.

QUARITCH, Mr., 15, Piccadilly, W.

RAINE, Rev. James, York.
RANKEN, Rev. W. A., Cuminestown, Turriff, N.B.
RAVEN, Rev. J. J., B.D., 17, South Quay, Great Yarmouth.
*REA, Charles,. Esq., Doddington Wooler, Northumberland.
†REDFERN, Rev. Robert S., Vicarage, Acton, Nantwich.
†REEVE, Henry, Esq., 62, Rutland Gate, S.W.
REFORM CLUB, Pall Mall.
REILLY, Francis S., Esq., 22, Old Buildings, Lincoln's Inn, W.C.
REYNELL, Charles W., Esq., 8, Hotham Villas, Putney.
REYNOLDS, Dr., The Cloisters, St. Michael's Hamlet, Liverpool.
*RIVINGTON, John, Esq., Redcliffe St. Mary Church, South Devon.
ROBERTS, Mr. Robert, Bookseller, Boston.
ROBINSON, W. L., Esq., Wakefield.
ROBSON, William, Esq., care of Dr. Robson, Warrington, Lancashire.
*ROOFE, William, Esq., Craven Cottage, Merton Road, Wandsworth.
ROSS, Henry, Esq., The Manor House, Swanscombe, Kent.
*ROSSETTI, W. M., Esq., 56, Euston Square, N.W.
*ROTHWELL, Charles, Esq., St. George's Place, Bolton.
*ROWE, J. Brooking, Esq., 16, Lockyer Street, Plymouth.
*ROYAL LIBRARY, Windsor Castle.
RUMNEY, Robert, Esq., Ardwick Chemical Works, near Manchester.
RUSKIN, John, Esq., Denmark Hill, Camberwell. (10 sets).
*RUSSELL, Thomas, Esq., 14, India Street, Glasgow.

ST. ANDREW'S UNIVERSITY LIBRARY.
ST. DAVID'S, Right Rev. Connop Thirlwall, Bishop of, Abergwili Palace, Carmarthen.
SALT, Samuel, Esq., Ulveston, Lancashire.
*SANDERS, S. J. W., Esq., 9, Lansdowne Crescent, Great Malvern.
SCHAIBLE, Dr. Charles H., 101, Gower Street, Bedford Square, W.C.
SCHWABE, Edm. S., Esq., Oak End, Halliwell Lane, Chetham Hill, Manchester.
SCHWABE, F. S., Esq., Rhodes House, Middleton, near Manchester.
SCOTT, James, Esq., The Lochies House, Burntisland, N.B.
SCOTT, William B., Esq., 33, Elgin Road, Notting Hill, W.
SHARPE, Samuel, Esq., Huddersfield College.
*SHIELDS, Thomas, Esq., Scarborough.
*SIMMONS, Rev. T. F., Dalton Holme, Beverley.
*SIMMS, Charles, Esq., King Street, Manchester.
SIMONTON, J. W., Esq., Harrisburg, Pennsylvania, U.S.
SINCLAIR, James B., Esq., 324, Dumbarton Road, Glasgow.
*SION COLLEGE, President and Fellows of, London Wall, E.C.
†SKEAT, Rev. Walter W., 22, Regent Street, Cambridge.
SLACK, John, Esq., Croft Lodge, Rothesay.

SLATTER, Rev. John, Streatley Vicarage, Reading.
*SMITH, Mr. Alexander, 214, New City Road, Glasgow.
SMITH, Charles, Esq., Faversham.
*SMITH, Toulmin, Esq., Wood Lane, Highgate.
SNELGROVE, Arthur G., Esq., London Hospital, S.
SNELL, Rev. W. M., Corpus Christi College, Cambridge.
SOLOMON, Saul, Esq., Cape Town, Cape of Good Hope.
*SPARK, H. King, Esq., Greenbank, Darlington.
SPRANGE, A. D., Esq., 12, Princes Square, Bayswater, W.
STANLEY, The Lord, 23, St. James's Square, S.W.
STEPHENS, Professor George, University of Copenhagen, Denmark.
*STEVENS, Brothers, Messrs., 17, Henrietta Street, Covent Garden. (2 sets).
STEVENSON, Rev. Professor William, D.D., 37, Royal Terrace, Edinburgh.
STEWART, Alexander B., Esq., Glasgow.
*STIRRUP, Mark, Esq., 62a, Mosley Street, Manchester.
STOCKHOLM ROYAL LIBRARY.
*STOKES, Whitley, Esq., Legislative Council Buildings, Calcutta.
*STONE, W. G., Esq., 40, High Street, West, Dorchester.
*STONYHURST COLLEGE, near Whalley, Lancashire.
STORR, Rayner, Esq., 26, King Street, Covent Garden, W.C.
STRATHERN, Sheriff, County Buildings, Glasgow.
STUBBS, Rev. Prof. William, North Parade, Oxford.
SUNDERLAND SUBSCRIPTION LIBRARY.
*SYMONDS, Rev. Henry, The Close, Norwich.

*TANNER, Dr. Thomas Hawkes, 9, Henrietta Street, Cavendish Square.
TAYLOR, Robert, Esq., Shrewsbury.
†TAYLOR, Thos. F., Esq., Highfield House, Pemberton, near Wigan.
TENNYSON, Alfred, Esq., D.C.L., Faringford, Isle of Wight.
TEW, Rev. Edmund, Patching Rectory, near Arundel, Sussex.
THOMPSON, Frederic, Esq., South Parade, Wakefield.
*THOMPSON, Joseph, Esq., Sandy Nook, Ardwick, Manchester.
THORNELY, John, Esq., 68, Chancery Lane, W.C.
*THORPE, Rev. J. F., Hernhill Vicarage, Faversham.
*TIMMINS, Samuel, Esq., Elvetham Lodge, Edgbaston, Birmingham.
TOD, John, Esq., 11, Rumford Street, Liverpool.
TOOLE, The Very Rev. Canon, Bedford House, Hulme, Manchester.
TROLLOPE, Anthony, Esq., Waltham House, Waltham, N.
TROLLOPE, T. A. Esq., Florence.
TROY, New York, Young Men's Association.
†TRÜBNER & Co., Messrs., 60, Paternoster Row, (80 sets.) *Extra Series.* 25 small and 1 large paper.
TURNER, Robert S., Esq., 1, Park Square West, Regent's Park, N.W.
TYSSEN, John R. D., Esq., 9, Rock Gardens, Brighton.

UNIVERSITY COLLEGE, LONDON, W.C.
*USHERWOOD, Rev. T. Edward, Uffington Parsonage, Shrewsbury.
*UTTOXETER LIBRARY, (care of James Potter, Esq., Hon. Sec.).

*VERNON, George V., Esq., Old Trafford, Manchester.
VIGFUSSON, Guðbrandr, 4, Clifton Villas, Cowley Road, Oxford.
VIZARD, John, Esq., Dursley, Gloucestershire.

WAKEFIELD BOOK SOCIETY.
„ MECHANICS' INSTITUTION.
WALES, George W., Esq., Boston, U.S.

WARD, Professor A. W., Owen's College, Manchester.
*WARD, Harry, Esq., British Museum, W.C.
WARWICK, John, Esq., 39, Bernard Street, Russell Square, W.C.
WATSON, Frederick Elwin, Esq., Thickthorn House, Cringleford, Norwich.
*WATSON, Robert Spence, Esq., Moss Croft, Gateshead-on-Tyne.
*WATTS, Thos,, Esq., British Museum, W.C. (2 sets and 1 *Extra Series*).
WAYTE, Rev. W., Eton College, Windsor.
WEBSTER, S. M., Esq., 33, Bridge Street, Warrington.
WEDGWOOD, Hensleigh, Esq., 1, Cumberland Place, Regent's Park.
WENT, James, Esq., Southlea, Malvern.
WEYMOUTH, R. F., Esq., Portland Grammar School, Plymouth.
*WHALLEY, J. E., Esq., 14, Marsden Street, Brown Street, Manchester.
WHEATLEY, Henry B., Esq., 53, Berners Street, W., *Hon. Sec.*
WHEELER, D. H., Esq., 17, Henrietta Street, Covent Garden, W.C.
*WHITAKER, J., Esq., 10, Warwick Square.
*WHITE, George H., Esq., 8, Bishopsgate Street Within, E.C.
*WHITE, Robert, Esq., 11, Claremont Place, Newcastle-on-Tyne.
WHITNEY, Henry Austin, Esq., Boston, Massachusetts.
WHITTARD, Rev. T. Middlemore, The College, Cheltenham.
WILBRAHAM, Henry, Esq., Chancery Office, Cross Street Chambers, Manchester.
WILKINSON, Dr. Alexander E., 10, Lever Street, Piccadilly, Manchester.
WILKS, Rev. T. C., Woking Parsonage, Woking Station.
WILLIAMS, Sydney, Esq., 14, Henrietta Street, Covent Garden, W.C. (4 sets.)
*WILLIAMSON, Rev. William, Fairstowe, Bath.
WILSON, Edmund, Esq., Red Hall, Leeds.
*WILSON, Edward J., Esq., 6, Whitefriars Gate, Hull.
WILSON, Lestock P., Esq., 37, Wigmore Street, W.
WILSON, Richard M., Esq., Fountain Street, Manchester.
*WILSON, Thomas, Esq., 2, Hillary Place, Leeds.
WIMPERIS, Joseph, Esq., 37. Ethelburga House, 70, Bishopsgate Street, E.C.
WINSTONE, Benjamin, Esq., 100, Shoe Lane, E.C.
*WINTERBOTTOM, Daniel, Esq., 35, Caledonian Road, Leeds.
WINWOOD, Rev. H. H. 4, Cavendish Crescent, Bath.
*WOOD, Rev. J. S., St. John's College, Cambridge.
WOODLEY, Frank, Esq., Middleton Park, Queenstown, Ireland.
WOODMAN, W., Esq., Stobhill, Morpeth.
WOOLLCOMBE, Rev. W. Walker, St. Andrew's Parsonage, Ardwick, Manchester.
*WREN, Walter, Esq., Wiltshire House, Brixton, S.
*WRIGHT, W. Aldis, Esq., Trinity College, Cambridge.
WRIGHT, Thomas, Esq., 14, Sydney Street, Brompton, S.W.

YOUNG, Alexander, Esq., 138, Hope Street, Glasgow.

SUBSCRIBERS TO THE EXTRA SERIES ALONE.

BAIN, T. G., Esq., 1, Haymarket.
HOPWOOD, G. B. Esq., 19, Trinity Street, Cambridge (Large Paper).
HUNT, W. P., Esq., Ipswich.
THRING, Rev. E., Head Master, Uppingham Grammar School.
TULK, John A., Esq., care of Mr. Bain, 1, Haymarket.

SUBSCRIBERS TO THE REPRINT.

For 1864 and 1865.

ARMSTRONG, H. C., Esq.
COLBORNE, W. H., M.D.
CONSTABLE, A., Esq,
DAVIES, W. Carey, Esq.
DAVIS, Henry, Esq.
DRAKE, W. H., Esq.
FOGO, D. F. Laurie, Esq.
FREEMAN, D. A., Esq.
HARBEN, Henry A., Esq.
HOWARD, Henry, Esq.
HYDE, J. J., Esq.
JENKINS, James, M.D.
MARTINEAU, Russell, Esq.
MONRO, J., Esq.
MUNTZ, G. H. M., Esq.
PECK LIBRARY, Norwich County, U.S.
POCOCK, C. I., Esq.
ROBERTS, Mr. R.
SCRIBNER, Messrs., New York.
SIMMONS, Rev. T. F.
SNELGROVE, A. G., Esq.
STEVENS, Messrs., Brothers.
UNIVERSITY COLLEGE, London.
WELFORD, Charles, Esq.

For 1864, 1865, & 1866.

ADAM, John, Esq.
ATKINSON, Rev. E., D.D.
BALTIMORE MERCANTILE LIBRARY.
BARRETT, Rev. Alfred, D.D.
BELL, Rev. W. R.
BLACKLEY, Rev. W. L.
BOTTOMLEY, Edward, Esq.
BRIDGES, Charles, Esq.
BURRA, James S., Esq.
CINCINNATI Public and School Library.
COCKIN, J. G., Esq.
COMPTON, Rev. Lord Alwyne
COX, Rev. Thomas
COXHEAD, A. C., Esq.
CULLEY, M. T., Esq.
DEIGHTON, BELL, & Co., Messrs.
EGGINTON, John, Esq.
ELY CATHEDRAL LIBRARY.
FROMMANN, Herr, Jena.
GINSBURG, Dr. Chr. D.
HARRIS, Mortimer, Esq.
HOUGHTON, Right Hon. Lord
HUNT, W. P., Esq.

For 1864, 1865, & 1866.

JACKSON, John, Esq.
KENRICK, William, Esq.
LAIDLAY, A., Esq.
MACLAREN, J. K., Esq.
MACMILLAN, Messrs., Cambridge (2 sets).
MARTINEAU, P. M., Esq.
NICHOLL, G. W., Esq.
NICOL, H., Esq.
NORRIS, WILLIAM, Esq.
NORWICH SCHOOL.
ODELL, A. J., Esq., New York.
ORMEROD, Henry M., Esq.
OXFORD AND CAMBRIDGE CLUB.
RAVEN, Rev. J. J.
ROSS, Henry, Esq.
ROTHWELL, Charles, Esq.
ROWE, J. Brookey, Esq.
SANDERS, S. J. W., Esq.
SAUNDERS, G. Symes, Esq., M.B.
SIMMS, Charles, Esq.
STONYHURST COLLEGE.
TANNER, T. H., M.D.
USHERWOOD, Rev. T. E.
UTTOXETER LIBRARY.
WEBSTER, S. M, Esq.
WESTHORP, C. Sterling, Esq.
WILKS, Rev. T. C.
WILLIAMS and NORGATE, Messrs. (2 sets).
WOOD, Rev. J. S.
WOODLEY, Frank, Esq.
WOOLCOMBE, Rev. W. W.

For 1864.

BRADFORD LIBRARY.
CHELTENHAM Permanent Library.
COMBE, Henry, Esq.
GRIFFITH, Rev. H. T.
RANKEN, Rev. W. A.
SLINGLUFF, C. B., Esq.
STIRRUP, Mark, Esq.

For 1865.

CHAMBERLAIN, A., Esq.
CHAMBERLAIN, Prof. J. H.
MUNBY, A. J., Esq.
TOOLE, Very Rev. Canon

For 1866.

CAPARN, Rev. W. B.
FALCONER, Thomas, Esq.
PENNSYLVANIA Historical Library.

Abstract of the Income and Expenditure of the Early English Text Society for the Year ending December 31st, 1867.

RECEIPTS.

	£	s.	d.
Balance at Bankers from last year's account...	31	10	0
Subscriptions :—			
1867. Three Hundred and fifty at £1 1s.	367	10	0
One hundred and thirty-four at £1	134	0	0
1868. Twenty	20	19	0
Payment for Ten Years in advance from Lord Stanley, 1868-77	10	10	0
Arrears ...	56	8	0
Sale of Texts (Trübner)	1	9	4
" (Ayenbite of Inwyt to members of the Kent Arch. Soc.)...	1	19	0
Philological Society (Extra for Ayenbite)	20	0	0
" (Share of Levins's Manipulus)	25	0	0
Camden Society (ditto)	48	2	6
Reprinting Fund :—			
Subscriptions for back years on Account...	62	16	0
Extra Series.			
Ninety-three Subscriptions for 1867 and 1868 ... 108 13 0			
Subscriptions from Percy MS. Fund... ... 52 10 0	161	3	0
	£941	**6**	**10**

PAYMENTS.

		£	s.	d.	£	s.	d.
Printing Account (Childs):							
No. 22. Parlenay (Extra)		4	11	8			
23. Ayenbite (Extra)		68	10	2			
24. Hymns to the Virgin		49	10	3			
25. Stacions of Rome		30	7	4			
29. Vision of Piers Plowman		107	3	4			
30. Pierce the Ploughman's Crede		49	15	2			
3500 Copies of Report		11	13	2			
Stitching various Texts		1	19	5	323	10	6
Ditto (Clarendon Press):							
No. 26. Religious Pieces...		40	16	9			
29. English Gilds (on account)		50	0	0	90	16	9
Ditto (Austin)							
No. 27. Levins's Manipulus		161	18	9			
H. Penfold, Esq. (Texts for 1865)		1	1	0			
Messrs. Trübner (Texts for 1864, '65, and '66)		3	0	0			
" " &c., (Delivery, Carriage, &c.)		14	5	5			
Petty Expenses:							
Copying Gilds, Troy, Piers Plowman, &c., &c.		87	16	0			
Postage, Stationery, &c.		8	15	1			
Extra Series:							
Printers on Account		110	0	0			
Purchase of Havelok, and Arthur of Britain for Reprinting		8	5	0			
Collating Caxton's Morte Arthur		9	3	0	127	8	0
Balance at Bankers		26	4	4			
" Extra Series		33	15	0			
" Reprinting Fund		62	16	0	122	15	4
					£941	**6**	**10**

We have examined this Account with the Books and Voucher, and certify that it is correct.

Wm. CUNNINGHAM GLEN, } Auditors.
REGINALD HANSON,

Myrc's
Instructions for Parish Priests.

DUBLIN: WILLIAM McGEE, 18, NASSAU STREET.
EDINBURGH: T. G. STEVENSON, 22, SOUTH FREDERICK STREET.
GLASGOW: M. OGLE & CO., 1, ROYAL EXCHANGE SQUARE.
BERLIN: ASHER & CO., UNTER DEN LINDEN, 20.
NEW YORK: C. SCRIBNER & CO.   LEYPOLDT & HOLT, 451, BROOME ST.
PHILADELPHIA: J. B. LIPPINCOTT & CO.
BOSTON U.S.: DUTTON & CO.

Instructions for Parish Priests.

By John Myrc.

EDITED FROM COTTON MS. CLAUDIUS A. II.,

BY

EDWARD PEACOCK, F.S.A., &c.

LONDON:
PUBLISHED FOR THE EARLY ENGLISH TEXT SOCIETY.
BY TRÜBNER & CO., 60, PATERNOSTER ROW.
MDCCCLXVIII.

HERTFORD:
Printed by STEPHEN AUSTIN.

PREFACE.

THE poem, now printed for the first time, has been preserved in at least three manuscripts. The best of these, as giving the earliest and purest text, is the one in the British Museum,[1] from which the present imprint is made. It was written out, in the editor's opinion, not later than the year 1450, perhaps a little earlier; but the language is of a somewhat older date. The other two manuscripts are among the late Mr. Douce's collections in the Bodleian Library.[2] These differ frequently, but seldom materially, from the London copy. They are of later execution, and shew a tendency to the vocabulary of the north country in their variations. They are not the handy-work of the same scribe, but the texts are so nearly identical that there can be little doubt that they have both been copied from one original. All the various readings that seemed of any interest have been noted. It was not desirable to record every difference of spelling.

Of the writer of the work nothing is known, except that he was a canon of Lilleshall, in Shropshire, a house founded by Richard de Belmeis, between 1144 and 1148, for a body of Arroasian canons. They were a branch of the order of canons regular of St. Austin, who took their name from the

---

[1] Cotton MS., Claud A. ii.   [2] Douce MSS., 60 and 103.

City of Arras, near which their first house, dedicated to St. Nicholas, was situated. The offshoot of which Mirk was in due time a member had, in its early days, many migrations. The first English home of the brotherhood seems to have been at a place called Lizard Grange. They afterwards occupied for a time some houses at Donnington Weald, from whence they moved to Dorchester, where they seem to have remained until their permanent home was fitted for their reception. Here they continued to reside until the suppression of the monastic orders. The site of the Abbey was granted by Henry the Eighth, in the thirty-first year of his reign, to James Leveson. Some remains still exist to shew that the church was a Norman building of fine proportions.[1]

Mirk was the author of another book, also in English, which is well worthy of the attention of those who take an interest in our earlier literature. A copy is preserved in the same volume from which this imprint is taken. Its title is *Liber Festivalis*. It consists of a collection of Sermons for the higher festivals of the Christian year, beginning with the first Sunday in Advent.

Mirk tells us that he translated this poem from a Latin book called *Pars Oculi*. Some people have therefore thought that it is a versified translation of John De Burgo's *Pupilla Oculi*. Such a suggestion can only have been made by persons whose acquaintance with the books was limited to their titles. De Burgo's book is probably twenty times as large, and is as different from Mirk's verses as a book well can be that treats in part upon similar subjects.

The *Manuale Sacerdotis* of Johannes Miræus, prior of Lilleshall, has also been conjectured to be the origin from which Mirk translated.[2] The prior's book is much like the monk's,

[1] Monast. Anglic, vi. 261 ; Coll. Arch., i 28; Pitseus, 577.
[2] There is a manuscript of this work in the Harleian Library, No. 5306.

both in subject and method of treatment; but it is much larger, and, in other ways, quite an independent work.

Although we cannot at present put our hands upon the original Latin text from which the version before us was made, it is quite evident that there is very little that is original about it. How could there be? The author was treating on subjects that were as old as the Christian church, and giving directions how priests with little book learning or experience were to teach the faith to their flocks. Great numbers of independent works of this nature were produced in the Middle Ages. There is probably not a language or dialect in Europe that has not now, or had not once, several treatises of this nature among its early literature. The growth of languages, the Reformation, and the alteration in clerical education, consequent on that great revolution, have caused a great part of them to perish or become forgotten.

A relic of this sort, fished up from the forgotten past, is very useful to us as a help towards understanding the sort of life our fathers lived. To many it will seem strange that these directions, written without the least thought of hostile criticism, when there was no danger in plain speaking, and no inducements to hide or soften down, should be so free from superstition. We have scarcely any of the nonsense which some people still think made up the greater part of the religion of the Middle Ages, but, instead thereof, good sound morality, such as it would be pleasant to hear preached at the present day.

The instructor tells his pupils of the great evil it is to have ignorant clergy, how instead of instructing their people they by their ill example lead them into sin. How their preaching is worth but very little if they tell lies or get drunk, are slothful, envious, or full of pride. How they may not without sin haunt taverns, or practice violent and cruel sports;

may not dance nor wear "cutted clothes and pyked schone;" nor go to fairs and markets, and strut about girt with sword and dagger like knights and esquires. On the other hand, he says priests must be gentle and modest, given to hospitality, and the reading of the psalter. They must avoid as much as may be the service of women, and especially of evil ones; eschew coarse jokes and ribald talking, and must be especially careful to shave the crown of their heads and their beards.

The priest must not be content with simply knowing his own duties. He must be prepared to teach those under his charge all that Christian men and women should do and believe. We are told that when any one has done a sin he must not continue long with it on his conscience, but go straight to the priest and confess it, least he should forget before the great shriving time at Easter tide. Pregnant women especially are to go to their shrift and receive the holy communion at once. Our instructor is very strict on the duties of midwives—women they were really in those days. They are on no account to permit children to die unbaptized. If there be no priest at hand, they are to administer that sacrament themselves if they see danger of death. They must be especially careful to use the right form of words, such as our Lord taught; but it does not matter whether they say them in Latin or English, or whether the Latin be good or bad, so that the intention be to use the proper words. The water and the vessel that contained it are not to be again employed in domestic use, but to be burned or carried to the church and cast into the font. If no one else be at hand, the parents themselves may baptize their children. All infants are to be christened at Easter and Whitsuntide in the newly blessed fonts, if there have not been necessity to administer the sacrament before. God-parents are to be careful to teach to their Godchildren the *Pater Noster*, *Ave Maria*, and *Credo*, and not to sleep in the same bed with them until they are old enough to take care of themselves, least they should be over-lain. Neither are they to be sponsors to their God-children at confirmation, for they have already contracted a spiritual relationship. Both the God-parents and those who have held the child at its confirming are spiritual relatives, and may not afterwards contract marriage with it.

Before weddings, bans are to be asked on three holidays; and all persons who contract irregular marriages, and the priests, clerks, and others that help thereat, are cursed for the same. The real presence of the body and blood of our Saviour in the Sacrament of the Altar is to be fully held; but the people are to bear in mind that the wine and water given to them after they have received Communion is not a part of the sacrament. It is an important thing to behave reverently in church, for the church is God's house, not a place for idle prattle. When people go there they are not to jest, or loll against the pillars and walls, but kneel down on the floor and pray to their Lord for mercy and grace. When the gospel is read they are to stand up and sign themselves with the cross; and when they hear the sanctus bell ring, they are to kneel and worship their Maker in the blessed sacrament.

Not a word is said by Mirk indicating that he knew anything about pews or even benches for the lay people. It is probable that these conveniences were not commonly needed at the time when he wrote.

All men are to shew reverence when they see the priest carrying the host and the sick. Whether the ways be dirty or clean they are not to think of their clothes, but reverently to kneel down " to worshype Hym that alle hath wroghte."

The author gives some very interesting instructions about

churchyards, which shew, what we knew from other circumstances to be the case, that they were sometimes treated with shameful irreverence. It was not for want of good instruction that our ancestors, in the days of the Plantagenets, played at rustic games, and that the gentry held their manorial courts over the sleeping places of the dead. That then, as seventy years ago,—as now perhaps—

> "dogs and donkeys, sheep and swine,
> The clerk's black mare, the parson's kine,
> Among the graves their pastime take;
> That at the yearly village wake
> Each man and woman, lad and lass,
> Do play at games upon the grass;
> Set curs to fight and cats to worry,
> And make the whole place hurry-skurry."

Of witchcraft we hear surprisingly little. Mirk's words are such that one might almost think he had some sceptical doubts on the subject. Not so with usury or "okere." The taking interest for money, or lending anything to get profit thereby, is, we are shewn, a "synne full greuus." This was the universally received teaching in his day, and for many centuries after. Perhaps the most remarkable fluctuation of opinion that has taken place in the modern period, is the silent change that has passed over men's minds on this important subject.

After these and several more general instructions of a similar character, almost all of them showing good religious feeling and clear common sense, the author gives a very good commentary on the Creed, the Sacraments, the Commandments, and the deadly sins. The little tract ends with a few words of instruction to priests as to the manner of saying mass, and of giving holy communion to the sick.

When the editor first read this little book, in one of the Oxford manuscripts, it was his intention to print it with an extended commentary, for the purpose of illustrating the ritual, religious, and social feelings of an important period in history. This would have been out of place in a publication of the Early English Text Society. The document as it stands speaks clearly enough to those to whom its voice is audible.

As an illustration of Mirk's work the editor has printed from Lansdowne MS., 762, seven questions to be asked of persons near death. The date of the manuscript from which they are taken is thought to be about 1470. The volume is partly written on vellum and partly on paper, and contains many different pieces. Several of them are prophesies.

The editor must not conclude without thanking his learned friend, John Ross, Esq., of Lincoln, for his many valuable notes and suggestions; especially for the interesting extracts concerning ankresses, from his unrivalled collections relative to the history of this his native county. He has also received kind help from the very Reverend Daniel Rock, D.D.; and from his friends James Fowler, Esq., F.S.A., of Wakefield, and the Reverend Joseph T. Fowler, F.S.A., of St. John's College, Hurstpierpoint.—E. P.

BOTTESFORD MANOR, NEAR BRIGG,
September 9, 1867.

ERRATA.

P. 22, l. 709, *scales* for *seales*.
P. 66, l. 28, *father and son* for *father to son*.

Instructions for Parish Priests.

Cotton. MS. Claudius A ii. Fol. 127.

¶ *Propter presbiterum parochialem instruendum.*

 God seyth hym self, as wryten we fynde,
  That whenne þe blynde ledeth þe blynde, *When the blind lead the blind both fall into the ditch.*
 In to þe dyche þey fallen boo,
4 For þey ne sen whare by to go.
 So faren prestes now by dawe;
 They beth blynde in goddes lawe,
 That whenne þey scholde þe pepul rede
8 In to synne þey do hem lede. *Priests lead their flocks into sin through their own want of lore.*
 Thus þey haue do now fulle ȝore,
 And alle ys for defawte of lore,
 Wharefore þou preste curatoure,
12 Ȝef þou plese thy sauyoure,
 Ȝef thow be not grete clerk, *Ignorant priests should read this book.*
 Loke thow moste[1] on thys werk;
 For here thow myȝte fynde & rede.
16 That þe be-houeth to conne node,
 How thow schalt thy paresche preche.
 And what þe nedeth hem to teche,
 And whyche þou moste þy self be.
20 Here also thow myȝte[2] hyt se; *Preaching worth little if the preacher's life be evil.*
 For luytel ys worthy þy prechynge,
 Ȝef thow be of euyle lyuynge.

  [1] oft.   [2] myghtest.

Priests must be chaste,	Preste,[1] þy self thow moste be chast,
	24 And say þy serues wyþowten hast,
	That mowthe & herte acorden I[2] fere,
	ȝef thow wolc that god þe here.
and eschew lies and oaths,	Of honde & mowþe þou moste be trewe,
	28 And grete oþes thow moste enchewe,[3] (sic)
	In worde and dede þou moste be mylde,
	Bothe to mon and to chylde.
drunkenness, gluttony, pride, sloth and envy.	Dronkelec[4] and glotonye,
	32 Pruyde and slouþe and enuye,
	Alle þow moste putten a-way,
	ȝef þow wolt serue god to pay.
	That þe nedeth, ete and drynke,
	36 But sle þy lust for any thynge.
They must keep from taverns, trading, wrestling, shooting, and the like.	Tauernes also thow moste for-sake,
	And marchaundyse þow schalt not make,
	Wrastelynge, & schotynge, & suche maner game,
	40 Thow myȝte not vse wythowte blame.
[Fol. 127 back.]	Hawkynge, huntynge,[5] and dawnsynge,
	Thow moste forgo for any thynge;
Cutted clothes, piked shoon, markets, and fairs to be avoided.	Cuttede clothes and pyked schone,
	44 Thy gode fame þey wole for-done.
	Marketes and feyres I the for-bede,
	But hyt be for the more nede,
	In honeste clothes[6] thow moste gon,
Armour not to be worn; beard and crown to be shaven.	48 Baselard ny bawdryke were þow non.
	Berde & crowne thow moste be schaue,
	ȝef thow wole thy ordere saue.
They must practise hospitality,	Of mete and drynke þow moste be fre,
	52 To pore and ryche by thy degre.
read the psalter, and take heed of domesday.	ȝerne[7] thow moste thy sawtere rede,
	And of the day of dome haue drede;
	And euere do gode a-ȝeynes euele,
	56 Or elles thow myȝte not lyue wele.

[1] ffirst.   [2] in.   [3] eschewe.   [4] Dronkelewe.
[5] Hawkes, houndes.   [6] clothing.   [7] Besely.

Wymmones serues¹ thow moste forsake,   *Priests should beware of women,*
Of euele fame leste they the make,
For wymmones speche that ben schrewes,   *and especially of shrews,*
60   Turne ofte a-way gode thewes.
From nyse iapes² and rybawdye,   *and avoid japes and ribaldry,*
Thow moste turne a-way þyn ȝe;
Tuynde³ þyn ȝe þat thow ne se
64   The⁴ cursede worldes vanyte.
Thus thys worlde þow moste despyse,   *that they may despise the world and follow after virtue.*
And holy vertues haue in vyse,
ȝef thow do þus thow schalt be dere
68   To alle men that sen and here.

Quid & quomodo predicare debet parochianos suos.

Thus thow moste also preche,   *What a priest must teach his flock.*
   And thy paresche ȝerne teche;
Whenne on hath done a synne,
72   Loke he lye not longe there ynne,
But a-non that he hym schryue,   *Shriving.*
Be hyt⁵ husbande be hyt⁶ wyue,
Leste he forȝet by lentenes day,⁷
76   And oute of mynde hyt go away.
Wymmen that ben wyth chy[l]de also,   *Women with child to go to confession,*
Thow moste hem teche how þey schule do.
Whenne here tyme ys neghe y-come,
80   Bydde hem do thus alle & some.
Theche hem to come & schryue hem clene,   [Fol. 128.]
And also hosele hem bothe at ene,   *and receive holy communion.*
For drede of perele that may be-falle,
84   In here trauelynge that come schalle.
To folowe the chylde ȝef hyt be nede,
ȝef heo se hyt be in drede;
And teche the mydewyf neuer the latere,   *The midwife's duties.*
88   That heo haue redy clene watere,

---

¹ felaship.   ² gaudees.   ³ Turne.   ⁴ This.   ⁵ he.
⁶ she.   ⁷ ester day.

Thenne bydde hyre spare for no schame,
To folowe the chylde there at hame,
And thagh*e* þe chylde bote half be bore,
92 Hed and necke and no more,
Bydde hyre spare neu*er* þe later
To crystene hyt and caste on water;
And but scho mowe se þe hed,
96 Loke scho folowe hyt for no red;
And ȝef the wo*m*mon thenne dye,
Teche the mydwyf that scho hye
For to vndo hyre wyth a knyf,
100 And for to saue the chyldes lyf
And hye that hyt crystened be,
For that ys a dede of charyte.
And ȝef hyre herte ther-to grylle,
104 Rather þenne the chylde scholde spylle,
Teche hyre thenne to calle a mon
That in that nede helpe hyre con.
For ȝef the chylde be so y-lore,
108 Scho may that wepen eu*er* more.
Bote ȝef the chylde y-bore be,
And in perele thow hyt se,
Ryght as he byd hyre done,
112 Caste on water and folowe hyt sone.
A-noþere way þow myght do ȝet,
In a vessel to crystene hyt,
And when scho hath do ryȝt so,
116 Wat*er*e and vessel brenne hem bo,
Othere brynge hyt to þe chyrche a-non,
And caste hyt in the font ston,[1]
But folowe thow not þe chylde twye,
120 Lest afterwarde hyt do the nuye.
Teche hem alle to be war and snel
That they conn*e* sey þe wordes wel,

---

[1] These two lines are not in Douce MS. 103.

THE DUTIES OF GODPARENTS.

And say the wordes alle on rowe
124 As a-non I wole ȝow schowe;
Say ryȝt thus and no more,
For nou othere wy*m*menes¹ lore;
¶ I folowe the or elles² I crystene þe, in the nome of   *The form of baptism*
128   the fader & þe sone and the holy gost. Amen.²
Or elles thus,² Ego baptiȝo te. N. In no*m*ino p*a*tris
  & filij & sp*iritu*s sa*n*cti   Ame*n*.
Englysch or latyn, whether me seyþ,   *may be said in English or Latin.*
132 Hyt suffyseth to the feyth
So that þe wordes be seyde on rowe,
Ryȝt as be-fore I dyde ȝow schowe;³
And ȝef þe cas be-falle so,
136 þat men & wy*m*men be fer hyre fro,   *The parents may christen the child if no one else be nigh.*
Then may the fader wyþoute blame
Crysten the chylde and ȝeue hyt name;
So may the moder in suche a drede
140 ȝef scho se that hyt be nede.
ȝet thow moste teche hem more,
That alle þe chyldren þat ben I-bore
Byfore aster and whyssone tyde,   *Children to be christened at Easter and Whitsuntide only, except of necessity.*
144 Eghte dayes they schullen a-byde,
That at the font halowynge
They mowe take here folowynge,
Saue tho that mowe not a-byde
148 For peryle of deth to that tyde.
A-nother tyme gyf hem folghthe
As the fader & þe moder wolþe.⁴
Godfader and godmoder þou moste p*r*eche   *God-parents to teach their godchildren pater noster, ave, and creed,*
152 þat þey here godchyldere to gode teche,
Here pater noster and here crede
Techen hem they mote nede.
By hem also they schule not slepe   *and not to sleep with them while very young.*
156 Tyl þey con hem self wel kepe.

¹ kynnes.   ² Not in Douce 103.   ³ myghtest knowe.   ⁴ þoȝte.

Confirmation.	Also wyth-ynne the fyfþe ȝere
	Do þat they I-bysbede were;
	For tho þat hydeth ouer more,
	160 The fader & þe moder mote rewe hyt sore;
	Out of chyrche schule be put
	Tyl þe byschope haue bysbede hyt.
[Fol. 129.]	And ȝet moste thow teche hem more,
	164 That godfader and godmoder be war be-fore,
God-parents not to hold their god-children at con-firmation.	¶ That they þat ben at the folowynge,
	Holde not þe chylde at the confermynge;[1]
	And also þow moste, as þou dost preche,
Relatives in blood by marriage or spiritually not to intermarry.	168 The cosynage of folowynge teche;
	And þow wolt that conne wel,
	Take gode hede on thys spel.
	In the myddel the chylde stont,
	172 As he ys folowed in the font.
	¶ Alle these be cosynes to hym for ay,
	That none of hem he wedde may;
Who are cousins by baptism.	The preste þat foloweþ, þe prestes chyldere, þe preste,
	176 And the chyldes fader & moder, þe godfader & hys
	Wyf knowe be-fore folghthe, þe godfader chylderen,
	the chyldes moder and hys godfader, &c.
	¶ The same cosynage in alle thynge,
	180 Is in the chyldes confermynge.
Who by confir-mation.	The chylde þat ys confermet,[2] þe byschop, þe
	byschopes chylderen, þe byschop and þe chyldes
	fader and hys moder, the godfader and hys wyf,
	184 the chyldes fader and hys godfader, the chyldes
	moder and hys godmoder,
	These schule neuer on wedde oþer,
	But cosynes beth as suster & broþer.
	188 Ȝet teche hem a-nother thynge,
Espousals.	That ys a poynt of weddynge;
	He that wole chese hym a fere,
	And seyth to hyre on thys manere,

[1] bisshoping. [2] Not in Douce 103.

MARRIAGE, AND LECHERY.

192 "Here I take the to my wedded wyf,   *Form of marriage.*
    And there-to I plyghte þe my trowþe
    Wyth-owten cowpulle or fleschly dede,"
    He þat wommon mote wedde nede;
196 For þaghe he or ho a-nother take,
    That word wole deuors[1] make.
    Loke also þey make non odde[2] weddynge,   *Irregular marriages are cursed.*
    Lest alle ben cursed in that doynge.
200 Preste & clerke and other also,
    That thylke serues huydeth so,
    But do ryʒt as seyn the lawes,
    Aske the banns thre halydawes.   *Banns to be asked.*
204 Then lete hem come and wytnes brynge   [Fol. 129 back.]
    To stonde by at here weddynge;
    So openlyche at the chyrche dore
    Lete hem eyther wedde othere,
208 Of lechery telle hem ryght þys   *Lechery a deadly sin,*
    That dedly synne for sothe hyt ys;
    On what skynnes maner so hyt be wroʒt,
    Dedly synne hyt ys forthe broght,
212 Saue in here wedhod[3]   *save in wedlock.*
    That ys feyre to-fore god.
    Thaʒ mon & wommon be sengul boþe,
    As dedly synne they schulen hyt loþe.
216 Also thys mote ben hem sayde,   *Children not to sleep together after seven years of age.*
    Boþe for knaue chyldere & for mayde,
    That whenne þey passe seuen ʒere,
    They schule no lengere lygge I-fere,
220 Leste they by-twynne hem brede
    The lykynge of that fowle dede.
    Also wryten wel I fynde,
    That of synne aʒeynes kynde
224 Thow schalt thy paresch no þynge teche,   *Pæderastia.*
    Ny of that synne no thynge preche;

---

[1] a dome.   [2] hond.   [3] wededhod.

Adultery is a great sin,	But say þus by gode a-vys,
	þat to gret synne forsoþe hyt ys,
	228 For any mon þat bereth lyf
	To forsake hys wedded wyf
	And do hys kynde other way,
	þat ys gret synne wyþowte nay;
which a man must confess to his shrift-father.	232 But how and where he doth þat synne,
	To hys schryffader¹ he mote þat mynne.
	Also thow moste thy god pay,
	Teche thy paresch þus & say,
	236 Alle that ben of warde² & elde
	þat cunnen hem self kepe & welde,
Confession.	They schulen alle to chyrche come,
	And ben I-schryue alle & some,
Communion to be received.	240 And be I-hoseled wyth-owte bere
	On aster day alle I-fere :
	In þat day by costome
	ȝe schule be hoselet alle & some.
[Fol. 130.]	244 Teche hem þenne wyth gode entent,
The real presence to be believed in.	To be-leue on that sacrament;
	That þey receyue in forme of bred,
	Hyt ys goddes body þat soffered ded
	248 Vp on the holy rode tre
	To bye owre synnes & make vs fre.
It is but wine and water that is given to the people after communion.	Teche hem þenne, neuer þe later,
	þat in þe chalys ys but wyn & water
	252 That þey receyueth for to drynke
	After that holy hoselynge;
Directions for receiving communion.	Therfore warne hem þow schal
	That þey ne chewe þat ost to smal,
	256 Leste to smale þey done hyt breke,
	And in here teth hyt do steke ;
Wine and water to be drunk after the host is eaten.	There fore þey schule wyth water & wyn
	Clanse here mowþ that noȝt leue þer In ;

¹ confessour.   ² wytte.

OF BEHAVIOUR IN CHURCH.

260 But teche hem alle to loue sadde,
  Þat hyt þat ys in þe awter made,
  Hyt ys verre goddes blode
  That he schedde on þe rode.
264 Ȝet þow moste teche hem mare
  Þat whenne þey doth to chyrche fare,
  Þenne bydde hem leue here mony wordes,
  Here ydel speche, and nyce bordes,
268 And put a-way alle vanyte,
  And say here pater noster & here aue.[1]
  No non in chyrche stonde schal,
  Ny lene to pyler ny to wal,
272 But fayre on kneus þey schule hem sette,
  Knelynge doun vp on the flette,
  And pray to god wyth herte meke
  To ȝeue hem grace and mercy eke.
276 Soffere hem to make no bere,
  But ay to be in here prayere,
  And whenne þe gospelle I-red be schalle,
  Teche hem þenne to stonde vp alle,
280 And blesse[2] feyre as þey conne
  Whenne gloria tibi ys by-gonne,
  And whenne þe gospel ys I-done,
  Teche hem oft to knele downe sone;
284 And whenne they here the belle rynge
  To that holy sakerynge,
  Teche hem knele downe boþe ȝonge & olde,
  And boþe here hondes vp to holde,
288 And say þenne in þys manere
  Feyre and softely wyth owte bere,
  "Ihesu, lord, welcome þow be,
  In forme of bred as I þe se;
292 Ihesu! for thy holy name,
  Schelde me to day fro synne & schame;

Side notes: The consecrated wine is God's blood that was shed on the rood. — How to behave in church. — Men should there put away all vanity and say the *pater noster* and *ave*. — Not to loll about, but to kneel on the floor. — When the Gospel is read all people are to stand up. — [Fol. 130 back.] They are to kneel when they hear the bell ring at the consecration. — A Prayer.

---

[1] crede.   [2] *add* hem.

Schryfte & howsele, lord, þou graunte me bo,
Er that I schale hennes go,
296 And verre contrycyone of my synne,
That I lord neuer dye there-Inne;
And as þow were of a may I-bore,
Sofere me neuer to be for-lore,
300 But whenne þat I schale hennes wende,
Grawnte me þe blysse wyth-owten ende.   AMEN."
Teche hem þus oþer sum oþere þynge,
To say at the holy sakerynge.
304 Teche hem also, I the pray,

All men are to kneel when they see a priest bearing the host.

That whenne þey walken in þe way
And sene þe preste a-gayn hem comynge,
Goddes body wyth hym berynge,
308 Thenne wyth grete deuocyone,
Teche hem þere to knele a-downe;
Fayre ne fowle, spare þey noghte
To worschype hym þat alle hath wroghte;

The benefits received by seeing the host, according to St. Augustinus.

312 For glad may þat mon be
þat ones in þe day may hym se;
For so mykyle gode doþ þat syȝt,
(As seynt austyn techeth a ryȝt,)
316 þat day þat þow syst goddes body,
þese benefyces schalt þou haue sycurly;[1]
Mete & drynke at thy nede,

The recipient on that day shall not lack food, shall be forgiven idle words and oaths, shall not [Fol. 131.] fall by sudden death, nor become blind.

Non schal þe þat day be gnede;[2]
320 Idele othes and wordes also
God for-ȝeueþ the bo;
Soden deth that ylke day,
The dar not drede wyþowte nay;
324 Also þat[3] day I the plyȝte
þow schalt not lese þyn ye syȝte;
And euery fote þat þou gost þenne,
þat holy syȝt for to sene,

---

[1] Douce 103 gives this line thus:—"Thou shalt haue þes sikerly."
[2] grede.   [3] thilk.

328 Þey schule be tolde to stonde in stede	
Whenne thow hast to hem nede.	
Also wyth-ynne chyrche & seyntwary¹	Games not to be played in church or churchyard.
Do ryȝt thus as I the say,	
332 Songe and cry² and suche fare,	
For to stynte þow schalt not spare;	
Castynge of axtre & eke of ston,	
Sofere hem þere to vse non;	
336 Bal and bares and suche play,	
Out of chyrcheȝorde put a-way;	
Courte holdynge and suche maner chost,	Courts not to be held there.
Out of seyntwary³ put þow most;	
340 For cryst hym self techeth vs	
Þat holy chyrche ys hys hows,	The church God's house.
Þat ys made for no þynge elles⁴	
But for to praye In, as þe boke telles;⁵	
344 Þere þe pepulle schale geder with Inne	
To prayen and to wepen for here synne.	
Teche hem also welle and greythe	
How þey schule paye here teythe:	Tythes to be duly paid,
348 Of alle þynge that doth hem newe,	
They schule teythe welle & trewe,	
After þe costome of þat cuntraye	
Euery mon hys teythynge⁶ schale paye	
352 Bothe of smale and of grete,	of small things and great, sheep, swine, and other live cattle.
Of schep and swyn & oþer nete.	
Teyþe of huyre and of honde,	
Goth by costome of þe londe.	It is useless to speak much of tithing, even ignorant priests understand that.
356 I holde hyt but an ydul þynge	
To speke myche of teythynge,	

¹ chirch hay.
² There is a note in Douce 103, f. 126b, in a hand a few years later than the text:—
"Danseyng, cotteyng, bollyng, tenessyng, hand ball, fott ball, stoil ball & all manner other games out cherchyard.
      I ye pra & reyng þat lent no be ther
      As it were in merket or fair."
³ churchyerd.   ⁴ moȝt elles.   ⁵ bookes.   ⁶ Eche one teythe.

Witchcraft forbidden.

[Fol. 131 back.]

Usury forbidden.

Men not to sell at too high a price.

Husbands and wives not to make vows of chastity, penance, or pilgrimage without the consent of each other.

  For þaȝ a *pr*este be but a fonne,¹
  Aske hys teyþynge welle he conne.
360 Wychecrafte and telynge,
  Forbede þou hem for any þynge;
  For who so be-leueth in þe fay
  Mote be-leue thus by any way,
364 That hyt ys a sleghþe of þe del³
  Þat makeþ a body to cache el.⁴
  Þenne syche be-leue he gart hem haue,
  Þat wychecrafte schale hem saue,
368 So wyth chames⁵ & wyth tele,
  He ys I-broȝte aȝeyn to hele.
  Þus wyth þe fende he ys I-blende,
  And hys by-leue ys I-schende.
372 Vsure and okere þat beth al on,
  Teche hem þat þey vse non;
  That ys a synne fulle greuus
  By-fore owre lord swete Ihesus.
376 God taketh myche on gref
  To selle a mon in hys myschef
  Any þynge to hye prys.
  For welle he wot þat oker hyt ys,
380 And lene .xij. d. to haue .xiij.
  For þat [is] vsure wyþowte wene.
  Teche hem also to lete one,
  To selle þe derrer for þe lone.
384 To preche hem also þou myȝt not wonde,—
  Bothe to wyf and eke husbonde,—
  Þat nowþer of hem no penau*n*ce take,
  Ny non a vow to chastite make,
388 Ny no pylg*r*image take to do
  But ȝef boþe assente þer to.
  These þre poyntes verement
  Nowþer schale do but boþe assent,

---

¹ fun. ² kon. ³ Or "de[ue]l." ⁴ Or "e[ue]l."
⁵ charmes: chames in the text is probably a scribal error.

392 Saue þe vow¹ to Iherusalem,   *Except the vow of a pilgrimage to Jerusalem.*
    Þat ys lawful to oþer of hem.
    Þenne schale þe husbonde als blyue²
    Teche & preche so hys wyue,
396 That heo a-vow no maner þynge   *Wives not to make vows unknown to their husbands.*
    But hyt be at hys wytynge;
    For þaȝ heo do, hyt may not stonde
    But heo haue grawnte of hyre husbonde;
400 And ȝef þe husbonde assente þer to,   [Fol. 132.]
    Þenne nedely hyt mote be do;
    No more schale he verement
    But hys wyf þerto assent.
404 The pater noster and þe crede,   *Pater noster and creed to be taught.*
    Preche þy paresche þou moste nede;
    Twyes or þryes in þe ȝere
    To þy paresch hole and fere,
408 Teche hem þus, and byd hem say
    Wyþ gode entent euery day,
    "FAder owre þat art in heuene,   *The "Our Father."*
    Halowed be þy name with meke steuene,
412 Þy kyngdom be for to come
    In vs synfulle alle and some;
    Þy wylle be do in erþe here
    As hyt ys in heuene clere;
416 Owre vche dayes bred, we þe pray,
    Þat þow ȝeue vs þys same day;
    And forgyue vs owre trespas
    As we done hem þat gult vs has;
420 And lede vs in to no fondynge,
    But schelde vs alle from euel þynge. Amen."
    "HAyl be þow mary fulle of grace;   *The "Hail Mary."*
    God ys wyþ þe in euery³ place;
424 I-blessed be þow of alle wymmen,
    And þe fruȝt of þy wombe Ihesus!⁴ Amen."

---

¹ avoue.   ² to stynt stryfe.   ³ eche a.   ⁴ MS. Ihc.

> "I be-leue in oure holy dryȝt,
> Fader of heuene god, almyȝt,
> 428 þat alle thynge has wroȝt,
> Heuene and erþe & alle of noȝt :
> On ihesu cryst I be-leue also,
> Hys only sone, and no mo,
> 432 þat was conceyued of þe holy spyryt,
> And of a mayde I-bore quyt,
> And afterward vnder pounce pylate
> Was I-take for vye and hate,
> 436 And soffrede peyne and passyone,
> And on þe croys was I-done;
> Ded and buryed he was also,
> And wente to helle to spoyle oure fo,
> 440 And ros to lyue the þryde day,
> And stegh to heuene þe .xl. day,[1]
> ȝet he schale come wyþ woundes rede
> To deme þe quyke and þe dede.
> 444 In þe holy gost I leue welle;
> In holy chyrche and hyre spelle.
> In goddes body I be-leue nowe,
> A-monge hys seyntes to ȝeue me rowe;
> 448 And of my synnes þat I haue done,
> To haue plenere remyssyone,
> And when my body from deth schal ryse,
> I leue to be wyth god and hyse,
> 452 And haue the ioye þat lasteþ ay;
> God graunte hym self þat I so may.   Amen."

The artykeles of the fey
 Teche þy paresch þus, & sey;
456 That seuene[2] to dyuynyte,
 And .vij. to the humanyte.
¶ *Primus.* The fyrste artykele ys þou wost
 Leue on fader and sone & holy gost.

---

[1] whan tyme he say.   [2] *add* perteyneth.

¶ ij*us*.   The secou*n*de ys to leue ry3t   2. The Father is
    461   þat þe fader ys god al my3t.   God Almighty.
¶ iij*us*.   The þrydde ys, as þow syst,   3. Jesus Christ is
          For to leue on ihesu cryst;   the Son of God,
    464   þat he ys goddes sone ry3t,
          And boþe on god & of on my3t.   and one with him.
¶ iiij*us*.   The holy gost, persone þrydde,   4. The Holy Ghost
          Leueth also, I 3ow bydde,   is God,
    468   That he ys god wyth oþ*er* two,
          And 3et on god and no mo.   and one with Fa-
          Leste þys be hard 3ow to leue,   ther and Son.
          By ensau*m*pul I wole þat preue:
    472   Se þe ensau*m*pul þat I 3ow schowe,   An illustration:
          Of water and ys and eke snowe;   water, ice, and
          Here beth þre þynges, as 3e may se,   snow are three
          And 3et þe þre alle water be.   and yet one.
    476   Thus þe fader and þe sone & þe holy gost   [Fol. 133.]
          Beth on god of my3tes most;   Thus it is with
          For þagh þey be person*us* þre,   the Father, Son,
          In on godhed knyt they be.   and Holy Ghost.
¶ v*us*.   These þre in on godhede   5. Who have made
    481   Wyth on assent and on rede,   with one assent
          Alle þyng*e* made wyth on spelle,   heaven, earth,
          Heuene, and vrþe, and eke helle.   and hell.
¶ vj.   The sexþe artykele, 3ef 3e wole fynde,   6. Power of the
    485   Holy chyrche taketh in mynde   Holy Ghost.
          That þor3 þe my3t of þe holy gost
          Is in vrthe of power most,
    488   And as my3ty, as I 3ow telle,
          Boþe of þe 3ates of heuene & helle
          To tuynen and open at heyre byddyng*e*
          Wythowte 3eyn-stondyng*e* of any þynge.
¶ vij*us*.   The seuenþe artykele, for soþe hyt ys,   7. The Resurrec-
    493   þat he schal ende in ioye & blys   tion.
          When body and soule to-geder schal come,
          And the gode to ioye be I-nome,

THE SEVEN SACRAMENTS.

	496 And the euel be put a-way
	In to the peyne that lasteþ ay.
8. Jesus Christ became man in Mary's womb.	¶ viij*us*. The eghþe artykele ys not to hele,
	þe strengþe of oure feyth þe more dele,
	500 The flesch and blod þat ihesus tok
	In mayde mary, as seyth þe bok,
	Þorȝ the holy gostes myȝt
	þat in þat holy vyrgyne lyȝt.
9. Who was a Virgin.	¶ ix*us*. The nynþe artykele ys for to mene
	505 þat he was bore of a mayde clene.
10. The Lord's passion.	¶ x*us*. þe tenþe artykele oure synne sleth,
	Crystes passyone and hys deth.
11. He went down into Hell, in soul and Godhead, while his body was in the tomb.	¶ xj*us*. The eleuenþe ys for to telle
	509 How he wente to spoyle helle,
	In soule and godhede wyth-owte nay
	Whyle the body in towmbe lay.
12. He rose again.	¶ xij*us*. The twelfþe artykele makeþ vs fayn,
	513 For he ros to lyue a-gayn
[Fol. 133 back.]	The þrydde day in the morowe
	For to bete alle oure sorowe.
13. He went up into Heaven on Holy Thursday.	¶ xiij*us*. The þreteneþe artykele, as telle I may,
	517 þat cryst hym self on holy þursday
	Stegh in to heuene in flesch & blod,
	That dyede by forn[1] on þe rod.
14. He shall come again at Domesday to judge the living and the dead.	¶ xiiij*us*. The fourteneþ artykele, ys soþe to say,
	521 þat cryst schale come on domes day
	Wyþ hys woundes fresch and rede
	To deme þe quyke and þe dede.
	524 Here ben þe artykeles of þe fey;
	Preche[2] hem ofte I þe prey.
The Seven Sacraments.	¶ *Septem sacramenta ecclesie.*
	TO preche also þow myȝt not[3] yrke
	þe .vij. sacramentes of holy chyrche.[4]

[1] bifor.   [2] Teche.   [3] die.   [4] kirk.

528 þat ys folghþe þat clanseþ synne,
    And confermynge after, as we may mynne,¹
    The sacrament of goddes body,
    And also penaunce þat ys verrey,
532 Ordere of prest, and spousayle,
    And þe laste elynge wyth-owte fayle;
    Lo here the seuene and no mo,
    Loke thow preche ofte þo.

I. Baptism.
II. Confirmation.
III. The Eucharist.
IV. Penance.
V. VI. Orders and Matrimony.
VII. Unction.

¶ *De sacramento baptismatis.*

Baptism.

536 ⸂Et I mote in thys worchynge
    Teche the more of folowynge,
    For hyt ys syche a sacrament
    þat may lyȝtely be I-schent
540 But hyt be done redyly
    In vche² a poynte by and by;
    Therfore do as I the say,
    Lest thow go out of þe way.
544 Hast þou wel vnderstonde my lore
    As I taghte the by-fore,
    How þou schuldest wymmen lere
    þat wyth chylde grete were?
548 But þys ys for þyn owne prow
    þat I here teche the now.
    Ȝef a chylde myscheueth at home,
    And ys I-folowed & has hys³ nome,

Children baptized at home to be brought to church.

552 Ȝef hyt to chyrche be broȝt to þe
    As hyt oweth for to be,
    Thenne moste þou slyly⁴
    Aske of hem þat were þere by,

[Fol. 134.]

The priest to ask those present at the baptism whether the words were said aright.

556 How þey deden þen in þat cas
    Whenne þe chylde I-folowed was,
    And wheþer þe wordes were seyde a-ryȝt,
    And not turnet in þat hyȝt;

¹ nym. ² euery. ³ no. ⁴ full sotelly.

560 ȝef þe wordes were seyde on rowe
As lo here I do þe schowe.

Ista sunt uerba baptismi in domo.

The words of baptism.

¶ I crystene þe, or elles I folowe þe, N. In nome of þe
fader and the sone, and the holy gost. Amen.
564 And þagh þou ȝeue no name to hem,
Ny nempne hem no man*er* name,
I telle hyt for no blame,
Hyt may be don al by thoght
568 Whenne hyt ys to chyrche I-broght,
And þaȝ, me say, as þey done vse
Sory laten in here wyse, (As þus)

Bad Latin spoils not the Sacrament,

I folowe þe in no*mina* p*a*tria & filia spirit*us*
572 sanctia. Amen.
Of these wordes take þow non hede,
þe folghþe ys gode wythoute drede
So þat here entent & here wyt

if the first syllable of each word be right.

576 Were forto folowe hyt;
Ay whyle þey holde þe fyrste sylabul
þe folghþe ys gode wythouten fabul (As þus)
Pa of pat*ris*. fi of filij. spi of spirit*us* s*an*cti. Amen.
580 Þenne do þe s*er*uyse neu*er* þe later,
Alle saue þe halowynge of þe water;

Holy oil to be used.

Creme & crysme and alle þynge elles
Do to þe chylde as þe bok telles;
584 And ȝef þe chylde haue nome by-fore,
Lete hyt stonde in goddes ore,
And ȝef hyt haue not, lete name hyt þare,
ȝef hyt schule in greyþe fare.

[Fol. 131 back.] If a person uses the matter and form of baptism in jest, it is not a sacrament unless he intended it to be so.

588 But what and on in hys bordes
Caste on water and say þe wordes,
Is þe chylde I-folowed or no?
By god I say nay for hem bo.
592 But ȝef hyt were hys fulle entent

To ȝeue þe chylde þat sacrament,
þenne mote hyt stonde wyþoute nay, (As þus)
And he þerfore rewe hyt may.

596 ¶ But ȝef cas falle thus,
þat he þe wordes sayde a-mys, *If the words are said in wrong order the sacrament is nought.*
Or þus In nomine filij & patris & spiritus sancti. Amen.
Or any oþer wey but þey set hem on rowe,
600 As þe fader & þe sone & þe holy gost,
In nomine patris & filij & spiritus sancti. Amen.
ȝef hyt be oþer weyes I-went,
Alle þe folghþe ys clene I-schent; *When the baptism has not been valid, the priest is to perform the holy rite over again,*
604 þenne moste þou, to make hyt trewe,
Say þe serues alle a-newe,
Blesse þe water & halowe þe font,
Ryght as hyt in bok stont;
608 þenne be þe war in alle þynge,
Whenne þou comest to þe plungynge,
þenne þou moste say ryȝt þus, *and say thus.*
Or elles þou dost alle a-mys,
612 ¶ Si tu es baptiȝatus, ego te non rebaptiȝo. Sed *Form of conditional baptism.*
si non es baptiȝatus, ego te baptiȝo. In nomine
patris & filij & spiritus sancti. amen.
þat oþer serues say þow myȝt
616 On þy bok alle forth ryght;
þow moste do þe same manere
ȝef a chylde I-fownde were, *A foundling is to be conditionally baptized.*
And no mon cowþe telle þere
620 Wheþer hyt were folowed or hyt nere;
þenne do to hyt in alle degre,
As here before þou myȝt se. *If a priest be so drunken that his tongue serves him not he must not baptize.*
But what & þou so dronken be
624 þat þy tonge wole not serue þe,
þenne folowe þow not by no way
But þou mowe the wordes say.
Luytel I-noghe for soþe hyt ys,
628 Thaghe thow be bothe war & wys, [Fol. 135.]

THE SACRAMENT OF BAPTISM.

      The sacrament for to do,
      Thaghe þou be neuer so abul þer to;
      How schulde þenne a droken[1] mon
632 Do þat þe sobere vnneþe con?
      And ȝef þow wole þy worschype saue,

Oil and creme to be always in readiness.

      Oyle & creme þow moste nede haue,
      Alway redy for ferde of drede,
636 To take þer-to when þou hast nede,
      And for to eschewe þe byschopus scheme,

Creme to be changed yearly.

      Vche ȝere ones chawnge þy creme,
      And þat as sone as thow may,

After Holy Thursday the oil to be changed.

640 A-non after schere þursday,
      Thow moste chawnge þyn oyle also,
      Þat þey mowe be newed bo,
      Ȝet wole I make relacyone
644 To þe of confyrmacyone
      Þat in lewde[2] mennes menynge

Confirmation

      Is I-called þe byspynge;
      But for þow hast þer of luytel to done,
648 Þer-fore I lete hyt passe ouer sone,
      For hyt ys þe bisschopes ofyce,
      I wot þe charge ys alle[3] hyse,
      But ȝet I wole seche ȝerne
652 Sumwhat þer of to make þe lerne.
      Þat sacrament mote nede be done,
      Of a bysschope nede as ston,

must be performed by a bishop.

No man of lower degree can perform it.

      Þer nys no mon of lower degre,
656 Þat may þat do but onlyche he.
      He confermeth & maketh sad.
      Þat at þe preste be-forn hath mad,

The name given in confirmation not to be changed.

      Wherfore þe nome þat ys þenne I-spoke
660 Moste stonde ferme as hyt were loke,[4]

The bonds to be left about the necks of children

      But ofte syþes þou hast I-sen
      Whenne þe chyldre confermed ben

---

[1] dronken.   [2] by englisshe.   [3] also.   [4] stoke.

THE FORM OF EXCOMMUNICATION.

  Bondes a-bowte here neckes be lafte,
664 Þat from hem schule not be rafte,
  Tyl at chyrche þe eghþe¹ day,
  Þe preste hym self take hem a-way.
  Þenne schale he wyth hys owne hondes
668 Brenne þat ylke same bondes,
  And wassche þe chylde ouer þe font
  Þere he was anoynted in þe front.
  And þagh a chylde confermet nere,
672 So þat he folowed by fore were,
  To dyspuyte þer of hyt ys no nede,
  He schale be saf wythowte drede.

who have been confirmed until the eighth day.

[Fol. 135 back.]

The child to be washed over the front on the eighth day.

THE WHOLE OF THIS SERVICE FOR EXCOMMUNICATION IS SUPPLIED FROM DOUCE MS. 103.

  Magna sententia pronuncienda.

  The gret sentence I write here,
676 That twies or thries in the yere
  Thou shalt pronounce, without lette,
  Whan thi parisse is togidir mette
  Thou shall pronounce this idous thing,
680 With crosse & candell and bell knylling
  Speke oute redely fir noȝt þou wond,
  That all mowe the understonde.

Excommunication to be pronounced two or three times a year.

with cross, candle, and tolling of the bell.

  Et tunc dicat isto modo.

The form of excommunication.

684 By auttorite of god almiȝti ffader & Son & holy gost,
  And of al þe Seyntes of heuen. ffirst we accursen al
  them that broken the pece of holy chirch or sturben
  hit; also all thilk that with hold eny fredomes of holy
688 chirch or beren awey, þat is to vnderstond londes,
  houses, rentes or fredomes or prokeren wher thorgh
  holy chirch is peyred. Also all thilk that for wrath

All persons are cursed that break the peace of the church,

or that rob the same;

¹ vij.

that withhold tithes, destroy them, bear them away, or consent thereto.		or for hate of eny *per*son or vicary propo*r* tithinges
	692	with holden, or destroyen with hem self or with her bestes, or beren awey, and all þat consenten thereto
		in heriny*n*g of the *per*son or of þe vicary or her
All slanderers,		pro*k*etours;[1] also all that vnrightfully defameth eny
fire-raisers,	696	*per*son or pr*o*kereth to be famed; also all that berneth holy chirch or eny o*þ*er place, and all þat co*n*senten
thieves, and receivers of stolen goods;		thereto; also all comon and opon theves, robbers, that agen the pes of the king robben and reven & slen and
	700	take away[2] eny ma*n*nys goode, and all her recepetoures
all heretics,		and co*n*sentoure*s*, also all heretikes þat don welyngly agen the lawe of holy chirche, and the feith of cristen dom, in worde or dede or counsaile, or in ensaumple,
usurers,	704	and all that[3] okereres & vsureres that by cause of
and such as lend out cattle in the hope of getting a higher price at pay-day than they could at loan-time;		wynnyng lene her catall to her eine cristen tyl a certen day for a mor pris þen hit mi3t haue be sold in tyme of lone; also all þat diffame man or woman wherfor
	708	her state and her lose is peyred, for envy or for hate;
forgers of Popes' bulls, and clippers of the king's money;		also all þat falsen the popes lett*r*es or billes or scales; also all þat falsen þe king*es* money or clippen it, also
users of false measures and weights;		all þat falsen or vse false measures, busshelles, galones,
	712	& potelles quartes [cuppes[4]] or false wightes, poundes or poundrelles, or false ellen yerdes, wetyngly o*þ*er þan þe lawe of þe lond woll; also all þat ordeyneth or
such as bear false witness against matrimony or testaments;		bereth false witnesse agen matrimony laufully made
	716	or agen testament that is true, by custom wetyngly;
all traitors and disturbers of the peace;		also all þat distroubleth þe pes of Engloud, and traitors that ben false or Isenting to falsenes, agen þe king or
stealers of holy things and destroyers of the church's goods;		the reame; also all þo that bereth awey holy thing
	720	oute of an holy place or vnholy þing fro[5] an holy place; also all þat distroyen corne or eny o*þ*er frutes that fallen to god or holy chirch in tounc or in felde, with bestes or with hondes wetyngly; also all that
all that help Jews or Saracens, or	724	helpen with strength, or with vitayles, or soccouren

[1] proctoures, Douce 60.   [2] ruyflen, Douce 60.   [3] Not in Douce 60.
[4] Added in Douce 60.   [5] sic, qy. error for "into."

Iewes or Sarȝons agen cristendom; also all þat sleen childeren, or distroyen boren or vnborn, with drynkes or with wichcraft, & all her consentes; also all þat
728 stondeth or herkeneth by nyȝtes vnder wolles, dores or wyndowes, for to spy touchinge euil, and all house brekeres & man quellers; also all þat comeneth with a *cu*rsed men or woman wetyngly; also all þat meyn-
732 teyn hem in her syn; also all þat maken false chartors or false eyres wityngly [also all þat maken expimentes or wichecrafte or charmes wi*th* oynementes of holy chirch, and all þat leben on he*m*; also all þat drawen
736 or with holden any teythinge*s* for wrath of eny man or falsely tichen¹] also all that layen hond on prest or clerk in violence or harme but hit hi*n* self defendant [or eny man in chirch or chirch yarde²] also all þo
740 that with drawen or with holden eny offeryng(*sic*) teything*es*; also all þat defoulen Seyntwary wherfor þe [holy³] office is withdrawe or church or churchyerd,⁴ most be newe hallowed, but they come to amendment; also all false
744 executores þat maken false testamentes and despose the goodes of him þat is dede oþ*er* wise than his will was at his departyng [or lette his biequest to chirch or to eny oþer place; also al þat leyen her childeren at eny
748 wey letes or at eny chirch dores or at eny other comyn weyes and leveth hem.⁵]

destroy children, born or unborn, with drinks or witchcraft;

all eavesdroppers, house-breakers, and man-quellers;

all such as commune wittingly with accursed persons;

all makers of experiments, witches, and charmers;

all that hold back tithes or strike priests;

all defilers of sanctuaries;

false executors;

and all that expose their children.

Isto modo pronunciari debet sentencia.   The sentence.

By the auc*thorit*e of the ffather and of the son and of the holy goost and of our lady Seynt Mary goddes
752 moder, of heuene, and all oþer virgines and Seynt mighele and all oþer apostles and Seynt Steven and all oþer martires, and Seynt Nicholas and all oþer confessoures & of all the holy hallowen of heuen; We
756 accursen and warren and dep*ar*ten from all gode dedes

We curse all

---

¹ Douce 60.   ² Douce 60.   ³ Douce 60.
⁴ churchay, Douce 60.   ⁵ Douce 60.

THE SENTENCE OF EXCOMMUNICATION.

who have committed the above-said crimes.

and preres of holy chirch, and of all þes halowen, and dampne into þe peyn of hell all þose þat haue don þes articles þat we haue seid bifore, till þey come to
760 amendment; We accursen hem by the auc*thori*te of the courte of Rome, within and withoute, sleping or waking, going & sytting, stonding and riding, lying aboue erthe and vnder erthe, spekyng and crying and
764 drynkyng; in wode, in water, in felde, in towne:

We pray the Father, Son, and Holy Ghost, and all saints, to curse them. May they have no part in the church's prayers, but may Hell be their meed, with Judas that betrayed our Lord.

acorsen hem fader and son and holy goost: accursen hom angeles and archangeles and all þe ix orders of heven; accursen hem p*a*triarkes prophet*es* and apostles
768 and all god*es* disapules and all holy Innocentes, martieres, co*n*fessoures & virgines, monk*es*, canons, heremytes, prest*es* and clerk*es* þat þey haue no p*ar*t of masse ne mat*en*es ne of none oþer gode praiers, that
772 ben do in holy chirch ne in none oþer places, but that þe peynes of hell be her mede with Iudas þat betrayed oure lorde Ihe*s*u Crist; and þe life of hem be put oute of the boke of lyfe tyll they come to amendment &
776 satisfaction made. fiat fiat. Amen.

Then the candle is to be thrown down, and the priest is to spit on the ground. The bells to ring.

Than þou thi candell shalt cast to grounde
And spet therto þe same stound
And lete also þe belles knylle
780 To make her hortes the mor grylle

Other causes for excommunication may be seen in the great charter and the charter of the forest.

Oþer poyntes ben many and fell
þat beth not well fore to hele
þat þou myȝt knowe thi self best
784 In the chartor of fforest
In þe gret chartor also
Thou myȝt se many mo.

De modo audiendi confessionem.

Confession and penance.

788 Now y praye þe take gode hede,
For þys þou moste conne nede,
Of schryfte & penau*n*ce I wole þe telle,
And a whyle þere In dwelle;

	But myche more þou moste wyten,	The shrift-father must know much more than is told here. He is to pray to God for wit.
792	Þenne þou fyndest here I-wryten,	
	And whenne þe fayleþ þer to wyt,	
	Pray to god to sende þe hyt,	
	For ofte þou moste penaunce ȝen	
796	Boþe to men and to wymmen,	
	Oþer weyes þen wole þe lawe	
	Leste they token hyt to harde on awe,	
	Hyt were fulle harde þat penaunce to do	Legal penances are very hard, and must be given discreetly.
800	That þe lawes ordeyneth to,	
	Therfore by gode dyscrecyone,	
	Þow moste in confessyone,	
	Ioyne penaunce bothe harde & lyȝte,	
804	As þou here aftere lerne myȝte.	
	But sykerly penaunce wyþowte schryfte[1]	Penance without shrift helps little the soul.
	Helpeþ luytel þe sowle þryfte;	
	Þerfore of schryfte I wole þe kenne	
808	And to ioyne penaunce þenne,	
	To here schryft þou moste be fayn,	
	And hye þerto wythowte layn.	
	And fyrst when any mon I-schryue wole be,	When a man goes to confession he is to kneel, and the priest is to ask him if he be of his parish.
812	Teche hym to knele downe on hys kne,	
	Fyrst þow moste aske hym þen,	
	Wheþer he be þy paresschen,	
	And ȝef he vnswere and say nay,	[Fol. 136.] If he be not, the priest may not hear his shrift unless he had leave to come from his own parish priest.
816	Theche hym home fayre hys way,	
	But he schowe þe I-wryten,	
	Where by þou myȝt wel I-wyten,	
	Þat he hath leue of hys prest	
820	To be I-schryue where hym lust,	A man may leave his parish priest and go to confession elsewhere for these reasons:—
	For these poyntes wyþowte nay	
	He may haue leue to go hys way,	
	And schryue hym at a-noþer prest	
824	Where that hym beste lust,[2]	

[1] These two lines not in Douce 103.
[2] The foregoing five lines not in Douce 103.

If his parish priest be indiscreet;	Leste indyscrete hys prest were,
	Hys confessyone for to here,
if he knew that his confession would be revealed;	Or ʒef he knewe by redy token
	828 Þat hys schryfte he wolde open,
if he had done a sin with any of the priest's near kindred, as mother, sister, concubine, or daughter;	Or ʒef hym self had done a synne
	By þe prestes sybbe kynne,
	Moder, or suster, or hys lemmon,
	832 Or by hys doghter ʒef he hade on,
if he feared that his priest would draw him into sin;	Or ʒef he stonde hym on awe,
	To dedly synne leste he hym drawe,
if he had made a vow of pilgrimage;	Or ʒef he hade vndertake
	836 Any pylgrymage for to make,
or if the priest had lain with any of his parishioners.	Or ʒef hys prest as doctorus sayn
	By any of hys paresch haue layn,
	For þese he may leue take,
	840 And to a-noþer hys schryfte make,
	And werne hym leue hys prest ne may
	Lest hyt greue hym a-noþer day,
	And þaʒ he do for noʒt hyt ys,
	844 Þe byschope wole ʒeue hym leue I-wys.
A priest may hear the confession of a scholar, a sailor, or a passenger;	Of scoler, of flotterer, or of passyngere
	Here schryft lawfully þou myʒt here;
	And also in a-noþer cas,
and if he has cursed any one he must absolve him.	848 ʒef þou a mon a-corset has,
	He mote nede be soyled of þe,
	Whoso pareschen euer he be;
	And of mon þat schal go fyʒte
He may also hear the shrift of a person about to go to battle;	852 In a bateyl for hys ryʒte,
	Hys schryft also þou myʒte here.
	Þaʒ he þy pareschen neuer were;
[Fol. 136 back.]	
or of one near death, though he be not a parishioner.	And of a mon þat deth ys negh.
	856 Here hys schryft but þen be slegh,
	Byd hym & oþer also by fore,
	ʒef þat þey to lyf keuere,[1]
	Þat þey go for more socour

[1] kore.

HOW TO HEAR CONFESSIONS. 27

860 To here owne curatour, — Penitents are to be bidden to go afterwards to their own curates and shrive them anew.
And schryue hem newe to hym bo
And take he penau*n*ce newe also.
¶ Or ȝef any do a synne,
864 And þy paresch be wyth Inne, — If any man sin in the parish,
Of þat synne a-soyle hym þenne,
Þaȝ he be not þy pareschenne,
But ȝef þe synne be so strong*e*,
868 To þe byschope þat hyt long*e*,
Or ȝef a mon be seruau*n*t, — or have an office there, his confession may be heard.
In þy paresch by couenau*n*t,
Or hath an ofyce or bayly,
872 Þat he ledeth hys lyf by,
And hys howseholde be elles where,
Pareschen he ys þenne þere,
Or ȝef any hath trowþe I-plyȝt — A person may be wedded who has plighted troth in the parish.
876 Wyþ-Inne þy paresch to any wyȝt,
Þenne þou myȝt hem wedden I-fere,
As hyt ys the court[1] manere.
But to þyn owne pareschenne
880 Do ryȝt þus as I þe kenne, — The priest is to teach his own flock to kneel. He is then to pull his hood over his eyes.
Teche hym to knele down*e* on hys kne
Pore oþer ryche wheþer he be,
Þen ouer þyn yen pulle þyn hod,
884 And here hys schryfte wyþ mylde mod.
But when a wo*m*mon cometh to þe, — When a woman comes to confession he is not to look on her face,
Loke hyre face þat þou ne se,
But teche hyre to knele down*e* þe by,
888 And su*m* what þy face from hyre þou wry,
Stylle as ston þer[2] þow sytte, — but to sit still as a stone;
And kepe þe well*e* þat þou ne spytte.
Koghe þow not þenne þy þonkes, — nor to spit or cough,
892 Ny wrynge þou not wyth þy schonkes,
Lest heo suppose þow make þat fare, — [Fol. 137.]
For wlatyng*e* þat þou herest þare,

[1] D 103, couthe.   [2] þen.

but to remain still as any maid.	But syt þou stylle as any mayde
	896 Tyl þat heo haue alle I-sayde,
When she hesitates,	And when heo stynteþ & seyþ no more,
	ȝef þou syst heo nedeth lore
	Þenne spek to hyre on þys wyse,
	900 And say, "take þe gode a-vyse,
he is to encourage her to speak boldly,	And what maner þynge þou art gulty of,
	Telle me boldely & make no scof.
	Telle me þy synne I þe praye
	904 And spare þow not by no waye,
	Wonde þow not for no schame
by saying he has perhaps sinned as bad or worse.	Parauentur I haue done þe same,
	And fulhelt myche more,
	908 ȝef þow knew alle my sore,
	Wherfore, sone, spare þow noȝt,
	But telle me what ys in þy þoȝt."
	And when he seyþ I con no more
	912 Freyne hym þus & grope hys sore,
	"Sone or doghter now herken me
	For sum what I wolc helpe þe,"
	And when þow herest what þow hast do
	916 Knowlache wel a-non þer to.

¶ *Hic incipit inquisicio in confessione.*

	Const þow þy pater and þyn aue
If the penitent does not know the pater, ave, and creed, he is to have such a penance set as will make him learn them.	And þy crede now telle þow me,
	ȝef he seyth he con hyt not,
	920 Take hys panawnce þenne he mot.
	To suche penaunce þenne þou hym turne,
	Þat wole make hym hyt to lerne.

¶ *Quod sufficit scire in lingua materna.*

	ȝef he conne hyt in hys tonge,
He is to be examined in the articles of the faith, and be asked—	924 To ȝeue hym penaunce hyt ys wronge,
	But of þe artykeles of þe fey
	Þus appose hym þenne & sey,

"Be-leuest þow on fader & sone & holygost,   *Believest thou in Father, Son, and Holy Ghost;*
928 As þou art holden wel þow wost
Thre persons in trynyte,
And on god, vnsware þow me,   [Fol. 137 back.]
þat goddes sone monkynde toke,
932 In mayde mary as seyth þe boke,   *In the Incarnation;*
And of þat mayde was I-bore,
Leuest þow þys? telle me by fore,
And on crystes passyone,   *on Christ's Passion and resurrection;*
936 And on hys resurrexyone,
And stegh vp in to heuen blys
In flesch and blod be-leuest þow þys,
And schal come with woundes rede
940 To deme þe quyke and þe dede,   *and his coming to judge the quick and the dead,*
And we vch one as we ben here
In body and sowle bothe I-fere,
Schule ryse at þe day of dome
944 And be redy at hys come,
And take þenne for oure doynge,
As we haue wroȝt here lyuynge,
Who so has do wel schale go to blysse,   *when the good shall go to bliss and the bad to pain!*
948 Who so has do euel to peyne I-wysse.
Be-leuest also verrely[1]   *Believest thou that it is God's own body which the priest gives at the houseling?*
þat hyt ys goddes owne body,
þat þe prest ȝeueth the,
952 Whenne þou schalt I-hoseled be,
Leuest also in fulle a tent,
How þat holy sacrament,
Is I-ȝeue to mon kynne
956 In remyssyone of here synne;
Be-leuest also now telle me
þat he þat lyueþ in charyte
Schale come to blysse sycurly,
960 And dwelle in seyntes cumpany.

[1] sadly.

EXAMINATION ON THE

The Ten Commandments.

Hec sunt .x. precepta dei.

Þe .x. cummawndementes of god almyȝt,
I wole the aske a non ryght,
And ȝef þou haue any I-borste,
964 Telle me a non þow moste.

I. Hast thou worshipped any thing above God?

¶ Hast þou worschypet any þynge
More þen god oure heuene kynge?
Hast þow lafte goddes name,
968 And called þe fend in any grame?

Hast thou had dealings with evil spirits, conjuring, or witchcraft, or [Fol. 138.] sorcery, or doubted any article of the faith?

Hast þow auy tyme I made coniurynge,
For þefte or for any oþer þynge?
Hast þow made any wych crafte,
972 For any þynge þat þe was rafte;
Hast þow made any sorcery
To gete wymmen to lyge hem by?
Hast þou had dowte, by any way,
976 In any poynt of the fey?

II. Hast thou taken false oaths, or sworn lightly?

¶ Seche þyn herte trewly ore
ȝef þow were any tyme forswore,
At court or hundret or at schyre,
980 For loue or drede or any huyre.
Hast þou be wonet to swere als,
By goddes bones or herte, fals,
What by hys woundes, nayles or tre,
984 Whenne þow myȝtes haue lete be?
Hast þou be wonet to swere ȝerne
For þynge þat dyde to noȝt turne?
Hast þow any tyme þy trowþe I-plyȝt,
988 And broken hyt a-gayn þe ryȝt?

III. Hast thou kept the Holy-days, gone to church, avoided work and riotous company?

¶ Hast þow holden þyn halyday,
And spend hyt wel to goddes pay?
Hast þow I-gon to chyrche fayn
992 To serue god wyþ alle þy mayn?
Hast þou any werke þat day I-wroȝt,
Or synned sore in dede or þoȝt?

	Be-þenke þe wel sone, I rede	
996	Of þy synne and þy mysdede.	
	For schotynge, for wrastelynge, & oþer play,	Shooting and other sports, going to the ale on holy-days, singing and rioting, injure the soul.
	For goynge to þe ale on halyday,	
	For syngynge, for roytynge, & syche fare,	
1000	þat ofte þe sowle doth myche care.[1]	
	þe halyday only ordeynet was,	Holy-days were ordained for God's service and to hear mass.
	To here goddes serues and þe mas,	
	And spene þat day in holynes,	
1004	And leue alle oþer bysynes	
	For a-pon þe werkeday,	
	Men be so bysy in vche way,	
	So that for here ocupacyone,	[Fol. 138 back.]
1008	þey leue myche of here deuocyone;	Men are so busy on other days that they have little time for devotion.
	Þerfore þey schule here halyday	
	Spene only god to pay;	
	And ȝef þey do any oþer þynge,	
1012	Þen serue god by here cunnynge,	
	Þen þey brekeþ goddes lay	
	And holdeth not here halyday.	
¶	Hast þow honowred by þy wyt	IV. Hast thou honoured thy father and mother?
1016	Fader and moder as god þe byt;	
	Hast þou any tyme made hem wroth,	
	In word or dede þat was hem loth;	
	Hast þou ȝeue hem at here nede	
1020	Mete & drynke cloþ or wede;	Hast thou given them meat, drink, and raiment at their need? Hast thou had prayers said for the repose of their souls.
	Ȝef þey ben dede & gon here way,	
	Hast þow made for hem to pray;	
	Hast þow done also honowre	
1024	To hym þat ys þy curatowre?	
	Leue welle sone in gode lewte,	
	I say not þys for loue of me,	
	But for þow owest to do honour	
1028	To hym þat ys þy curatour.[2]	

[1] D 103, That moche agen the soule are.
[2] The foregoing four lines are not in Douce 103 or 60.

V. Hast thou slain	¶ Hast þow any mon I-slayn,
	Or holpe þer to by þy mayn;
	Hast þou counceled or ȝeue mede
	1032 To any mon to do þat dede?
or wounded any one?	Hast þou any mon wowndet in debate,
	Or had to hym any dedly hate?
	¶ Hast þou ȝeue any mon of þy mete,
Hast thou slain any one's soul by bad example?	1036 When he hade hongur and nede to ete?
	By euel esaumpulle þow myȝt also,
	A-noþer monnes sowle slo;
	Þerfore take hede on þy lyuynge
	1040 Ȝef þou haue trespaset in syche þynge.
VI. Hast thou put away thy wife, or otherwise sinned against chastity?	¶ Hast þou in synne I-lad þy lyf,
	And put a-way þyn owne wyf;
	Hast þou I-do þat ylke synne
	1044 To any of þy sybbe kynne?
[Fol. 139.]	Take also wel in mynde,
	Ȝef þou haue sched þyn owne kynde,
	Slepynge or wakynge nyȝt or day
	1048 In what maner þow moste say.
VII. Hast thou stolen anything, or been at a robbing;	¶ Hast þou stolen any þynge,
	Or ben at any robbynge;
	Hast þou by maystry or by craft,
	1052 Any mon hys good be-raft;
	Hast þou I-founde any þynge
	And helet hyt at askynge;
used false measures or weights;	Hast þou vset mesures fals,
	1056 Or wyghtes þat were als
	By þe more to bye & by þe lasse to selle?
	Ȝef þou haue so done þow moste hyt telle;
borrowed things and not returned them, or withholden tithes?	Hast þou borowet oght wel fayn,
	1060 And not I-quyt hyt wel a-gayn
	Hast þou wyth-holden any teyþynge,
	Or mys-I-teyþed by þy wytynge.
VIII. Hast thou borne false witness or got anything by perjury?	¶ Hast þow boren any wytnes
	1064 A-gayn þe ryȝt in falsnes.

Hast þow lyct any lesyngₑ,
To greue any mon in any þyngₑ?
Hast þou geten wyth fals swore¹
1068 Any þyngₑ lasse or more?

¶ Hast þou I-coueted wyþ alle þy myȝt,
þy neghbores good agayn þe ryȝt;
Hows² or catel, hors or mare,
1072 Or oght þat he myȝt euel spare?

IX. Hast thou coveted thy neighbour's goods, his house, cattle, horse, or mare!

¶ Also þou dost syngen ylle,
þy neghbores wyf for to wylle,
For þat god for-bedeþ the.

X. Thou sinnest ill if thou wishest for thy neighbour's wife.

1076 ȝef þou haue done, now telle þou me.
þow myȝte synge als sore in þoght,
As þou þat dede hudest I-wroght,
ȝef þow in þy þoght haue lykyngₑ
1080 To do þat ylke fowle þyngₑ.
þus þow myȝte synge dedlyche
ȝef þow þenke þer-on myche,

The desire to do evil is itself a sin.

These ben þe cummawndementes ten,
1084 þat god ȝaf to alle men.

[Fol. 139 back.]

¶ *De modo inquirendi de .vij. peccatis mortalibus.*

Of dedly synnes now also,
I wole þe aske now er þow go.
þerfore sone spare þow noght,
1088 To telle how þou hast hem wroȝt.

Of deadly sins.

¶ *De superbia.*

Hast þou any tyme wytyngly,
I-wrathþad þy god greuowsly?
Hast þow ben inobedyent
1092 A-gayn goddes cummawndement?
Hast þou for pruyde I-set at noght
Hym þat hath þe gode I-taght?

Hast thou, knowingly, made God angry;

for pride despised him who has taught thee good?

---

¹ ware.   ² cowe.

        Hast þou any tyme bost I-mad,
1096 Of any good þat þou hast had
        Only of þyn owne wyt,
        When god hym self ȝaf þe hyt?
        Hast thow forsake þyn owne gult,

Hast thou laid the blame of thine own sin on another?

1100 And on a-noþer þe blame I-pult?
        Hast þou feynet the holy
        By ypocryse and foly?
        Hast þou any tyme I-feynet þe

Hast thou pretended to be holy to hide sin and pride?

1104 Gode and holy on to se,
        In hope on þat maner to huyde
        Boþe þy synne and þy pruyde?
        Hast þow any tyme I-take on þe

Hast thou passed off others' good deeds as thine own,

1108 Any gode dede of charyte
        Þat was a-noþer monnes doynge,
        And of þyn no maner þynge?
        Hast þow ay oppresset þy neghbour

or oppressed thy neighbour to get honour;

1112 For to gete þe honour?
        Hast þou I-schend hys gode fame
        For to gete þe a gode name?
        Hast þou also prowde I-be

or been proud of thy virtues, thy voice, thy wit, thy hair, thy body, or thy strength;

1116 Of any vertu þat god ȝaf þe?
        For þy voys was gode & hye.
        Or for þy wyt was gode & slye,

[Fol. 140.]

        Or for hys[1] herus were cryspe & longe,
1120 Or for þow hast a renabulle[2] tonge,
        [Or for thy body is fayr and long,
        Or for þou art white & strong,[3]]
        Or for þy flesch ys whyte and clene,
1124 Or any syche degre to say at ene?
        Hast þou be prowde and eke of port

or that thou art trusted by lady or lord, or that thou comest of high family?

        For tryste of lady and eke of lord?
        Hast þou be prowde of worschype or gode,
1128 Or for þow come of grete blode?

---

[1] thy. [2] resonable. [3] Not in Cotton. MS.

> Hast þou any tyme þe prodder þe mad,
> For any ofyce þat þow hast had?
> Hast þow be prowde gostely?
> 1132 Telle me, sone, baldely.
> Of mekenes of pacyens or of pyte,
> Of pouert of largenes or of chastyte,
> And oþer vertues mony mo
> 1136 Wayte¹ lest þou haue synget in þo.
> Hast þow any tyme wyth herte prowd
> A-noþeres synne I-spoken owt,
> And þyn entencyone syche was,
> 1140 Þat þy synne schulde seme þe las?
> Hast þou ben prowde & glad in thoght
> Of any mysdede þat þou hast wroȝt?
> Hast þou ben prowde of any gyse
> 1144 Of any þynge þat þou dedust vse,
> Of party hosen of pykede schone,
> Of fytered cloþes as foles done,
> Of londes rentes of gay howsynge,
> 1148 Of mony seruauntes to þy byddynge,
> Or of hors fat and rownde,
> Or for þy godes were hole & sownde,
> Or for þow art gret and ryche
> 1152 Þat no neȝbore ys þe I-lyche,
> Or for þow art a vertues² mon,
> And const more þen a-noþer con?
> Ȝef þou haue be on þys maner prowd,
> 1156 Schryf þe sone and telle hyt out.
> Hast þou any tyme by veyn glory
> I þoght þy self so holy,
> Þat þow hast had any dedeyn
> 1160 Of oþer synfulle þat þou hast seyn?

Hast thou been proud on account of any office that thou hast held?

Hast thou made public another's sin,

or been proud of thine own sins,

or of thy dress, as fools are wont to be,

or of thy goods, or thy riches,

thy virtue or thy knowledge?

[Fol. 140 back.]

Hast thou despised others for being less holy than thyself?

---

¹ ware. ² crast.

¶ De accidia.

[Marginal notes:]
Hast thou been slow to teach thy godchildren?
Hast thou come to church late, and spoken of sin at the gate?
Hast thou hindered others from going to church, or spoken harlotry within the sanctuary?
Hast thou heard sermons without devotion,
or been loth to fast,
or do works of charity?
Hast thou neglected pilgrimage?

  HAst þou be slowe & take non hede,
   To teche þy godchyldre pater noster & crede?
  Haste þow be slowe for to here,
1164 Goddes serues when tyme were?
  Hast þou come to chyrche late
  And spoken of synne by þe gate?
  Hast þou be slowe to goddes seruyse,
1168 Or storbet hyt by any wyse?
  Hast þou letted any mon
  Þat to chyrche wolde haue gon?
  Hast þow spoken harlatry
1172 Wythynne chyrche or seyntwary?
  Hath þy herte be wroth or gret
  When goddes serues was drawe[1] on tret?
  Hast þow hyet hyt to þe ende
1176 Þat þou myȝtes hamward wende?
  Hast þow wyþowte deuocyone
  I-herde any predycacyone?
  Hast þou gon or seten elles where
1180 When þou myȝtest haue ben þere?
  Hast þou be slowe & loth to faste,
  When þy herte þere-a-ȝeyn[2] dyde caste?
  Hast þou be slowe in any degre
1184 For to do werke of charyte?
  Hast þou be slowe & feynt in herte
  To do penaunce for hyt dyde smerte?
  Hast þou any pylgrimage laft vn-do
1188 When þou were I-ioynet þer-to?
  Hast þow by-gunne any dede,
  For goddus loue and sowle nede,
  Prayerus, penaunce, or fastynge,
1192 Or any oþer holy thynge,

---

[1] seid.   [2] þus to.

OF ENVY. 37

  And afterward were so slowe and feynt,   [Fol. 141.]
  Þat þy deuocyone were alle I-queynt?
  Hast þow slowe & feynt I-be   Hast thou been slow to help thy
1196 To helpe þy wyf & þy meyne   wife to what she had need of?
  Of suche as þey hade nede to?
  Sey ȝef þow haue, so I-do.
  Ȝef þow be a seruaunt,   If thou art a servant, hast thou
1200 Hast þow holde þy couenaunt?   done thy duty to thy master?
  Hast þow be scharpe and bysy
  To serue þy mayster trewely?
  Hast þow trewely by vche way
1204 Descruet þy mete & þy pay?
  Hath thy neghbore I-trust to þe   Hast thou done thy duty to thy
  To helpe hym in any degre,   neighbour in those matters
  And þow for slowthe & feyntyse   wherein he trusted thee?
1208 Hast hym be-gylet in any wyse?
  Hath slowþe so I-schent þy þoȝt,   Hast thou given way to despair?
  Þat in dyspayre hyt hath þe broȝt,
  And neuer myȝtest þou non ende make
1212 Of no gode dede þat þou dydest take?
  Hast þou for slowþe I-be so feynt,   Hast thou given way to sloth, or
  Þat al þy wylle has be weynt,   neglected to go to church for
  And soȝt no þynge elles but lust & ese,   heat or cold?
1216 And alle þat wolde þy body plese?
  Hast þou spared for hete or colde
  To go to chyrche when þou were holde?

    ¶ *De invidia.*

  Hast þow euer be gruchynge   Hast thou had a grudge against
1220   A-gaynes god for any þynge?   God for anything, or been glad when
  Hast þow be in herte glad,   thy neighbour came to harm?
  When þy neghbore harme hath had?
  Hast þow had in herte gref
1224 Of hys gode and hys relef?
  Hast þow had enuye and erre   Hast thou envied thy betters,
  To hym þat was þyn ouer herre,

Or any þat was in any degre
1228 I-take forth by-fore the?
Hast thow enuyet þyn euenynge
For he had euer in any þynge,
Or for he was more abeler þen þow
1232 To alle manere gode and prow?
Hast þow enuyet þyn vnderlynge,
For he was gode and thryuynge,
Or leste he hade I-passed þe
1236 In any vertu or degre?
Hast þow for hate or for enuye
I-holpen or counselet for to lye
Any mon for to defame,
1240 Or for to destruye hys gode name?
Hast þow bacbyted þy neghbore
For to make hym fare þe worre?
Hast þow reret any debate
1244 A-monge þy neȝborus by any hate?
Hast þow I-sparet for enuye
To teche a mon hys harme to flye,
When þow myȝtest by þy warnynge
1248 Haue hym saued from harmynge?

De ira.

Hast þow for hate or for yre,
  Any þyngus set on fuyre?
Hast þow any tyme be wroth so
1252 þat þy wyt hath be a-go?
Hast þou by malys of þy doynge
Wrathþed þy neȝbore in any þynge?
Hast þow in wrathþe and wyth stryf
1256 I-greuet any crystene lyf?
Hast þow wyþ wordes bytter & schrewede
I-tened any mon lered or lewede?
Hast þow in wraþþe & euel herte
1260 I-made any mon to smerte?

Hast þow I-corsed or I-blamet,
Or any mon to wrathþe I-taimet?
Hast þow in wraþþe any mon slayn,
1264 Or holpe þer-to by thy mayn?
Hast þow be wonet to speke ylle
By any mon lowde or stylle?
Hast þow be glad to here bacbyte,
1268 Any mon myche or luyte?
Hast þou any tyme in malencoly
I-corset any þynge bytterly,
In hope to make hyt fare þe worse
1272 By þe malys of thy corse?
Hast þow be inpacyent
For any gref that god þe sent;
Or elles I-gruched a-gaynes hyt,
1276 In herte or worde oþer in wyt,
As ȝef þy catell fel from the,
Oþer for any infyrmyte,
For los of frendes or of any þynge
1280 Or for any syche doynge?

Hast thou slain any one in thine anger?

[Fol. 142.]

Hast thou been glad to listen unto backbiting?

Hast thou cursed anything in thy melancholy, in hope to make it fare worse?

Hast thou been impatient at loss of cattle or of friends?

De auaricia.

Hast þow wylnet by couetyse
Worldes gode ouer syse,
And spared nother for god ny mon
1284 To gete þat þow fel vp-on?
Hast thow be hard and nythyꝛge
To wythholden any thynge?
Hath any mon vp-on a wedde
1288 Borowet at the oght in nede,
And afterward when he pay wolde,
Hast þow þenne hys wed wythholde?
For þagh he fayle of hys day,
1292 Þow schuldest not hys wed wyþ-say.
Hast þow I-land any thynge
To haue the more wynnynge?

Hast thou been greedy of gain?

Hast thou been hard with borrowers,

or lent anything to gain profit thereby?

Hast thou practised simony?

Hast thou beguiled anyone in bargaining?

Hast thou given any false award to gain by it,

or perjured thyself for the same?

[Fol. 142 back.]

Hast thou coveted over much the world's worship?

Hast thou been an executor and neglected to do the dead person's will?

Hast thou been guilty of gluttony,

or eaten so greedily that thou hast vomited?

Hast thou in such vomiting cast up the holy eucharist?

Hast thou often been drunken,

or made others drunk that thou mightest beguile them out of anything,

or pick sport out of them?

   Hast þow I-dronke[1] symonye
1296 Spyrytual þynge to selle or bye?
   Hast þow werkemen oght wyth-tan
   Of any þynge þat þey schulde han?
   Hast þow by-gylet in chafare
1300 Any lyf in lasse or mare?
   Hast þow ȝeue a fals dome
   For any mede þat þe come?
   Hast þow falsly be for-swore
1304 For any þyng þow couetest ȝore?
   Hast þow I-gete any thynge
   Wyth fals countenans and glosynge?
   Hast þow I-coueted ouer gate
1308 Worldes worschype or any a-state?
   Hast þou I-be any executour
   To any frende or neghbour,
   And drawe out hys gode þe tylle,
1312 And not I-do þe dedes wylle?

De gula.

   Hast þou I-synget in glotorye?
   Telle me, sone, baldelye.
   Hast þow ete wyth syche mayn,
1316 Þat þow hast caste hyt vp a-gayn?
   Hast þow wyþ suche vomysment
   I-cast vp a-ȝayn þe sacrament?
   Hast þow be dronke ofte by vse,
1320 And schent þy self by þat vyce?
   Hast þou by malys or by nyste
   I-made any mon dronke to be,
   For þou woldest þe mene whyle
1324 Any þynge of hym by-gyle,
   Or for þow woldest borde[2] haue,
   To se hym dronke and to raue?

---

[1] y do.   [2] laughter.

  Hast þou I-fast as þou schuldest do,   *Hast thou fasted*
1328 Dayes þat þow were ioynct to,   *at proper times?*
  Or any oþer fastynge day?
  ȝef þow haue do þou moste say.
  Hast þow also for glotory
1332 Ete or dronke to frechedely?¹   *Hast thou eaten*
  Hast þow ete or dronke more,   *and drunken*
  Þen þy nede askede fore,   *more than need*
  Oþer to erly or to late,   *were?*
1336 Oþer to swete or delycate?
  ȝef þow haue done þus by vys,
  Telle me, sone, for nede hyt ys.
  Hast þow I-chereschet þy body ofte,   *Hast thou cher-*
1340 In swete metus and cloþus softe?   *ished thy body with sweet meat and soft clothing?*
  Art þow I-wonet to go to þe ale,   *Art thou wont to*
  To fulle þere thy fowle male,   [Fol. 143.]
  And drawe þyder oþer wyth þe,   *go to the ale to play the glutton?*
1344 To bere þe feleschype in þat degre?
  Hast þou I-stole mete or drynke,   *Hast thou stolen*
  For þou woldest not þerfore swynke?   *meat or drink?*

¶ *De luxuria.*

  Hast þow synged in lechery?   *Hast thou sinned*
1348   Telle me sone baldely;   *in lechery?*
  And how ofte þow dydest þat dede,
  Telle me þow moste nede;
  And wheþer hyt were wyf or may,   *and was it with*
1352 Sybbe or fremde þat þow by lay;   *wife, maiden, or kindred;*
  And ȝef ho were syb to the,
  How syb þow moste telle me;
  And ȝe[f] ho were ankeras or nonne,   *with ankeress,*
1356 Wydowe or wyf telle ȝef þou conne,   *nun, widow, or any woman vow-*
  Or any þat haþ a-vowet to chastyte,   *ed to chastity,*
  Or comyn wommon ȝef ho be,   *or with a common woman?*

---

¹ fresshly.

Was it with the woman's consent?	Or wheþer þow dost by strengþe so, 1360 Or by asent of ȝow bo?
Hast thou eaten or drunken anything to enforce to lust?	Hast þou ete or dronke any letewary To enforce the to lechery? Hast þow any þynge wroȝt or do, 1364 Þat stered þy flesch þe more þerto,
Kissing.	Clyppynge, or kyssynge, or towchynge of lyth, That thy flesch was styred wyth? Hast þow be tempted to any wommon,
	1368 And myche & ȝerne I-þoght þer-on,
Hast thou much desired to commit this sin,	And woldest fayn in thy þoght, Þat fowle dede wyþ hyre haue wroȝt? Þen þow dost synne in lechery, 1372 As god hym self seyth verroly, Wythowte werke or fleschly dede Þy chastyte from þe doth flede. Hast þow had lust inwardely,
and thought much on lechery!	1376 And þoȝt myche in lechery, And hast be tempted in syche a þoȝt? Telle me, sone, spare þow noȝt.
[Fol. 143 back.]	Slepynge or wakynge wheþer hyt were, 1380 Telle me, sone, a-non ryght here. Hast þow do sorfet of mete & drynke, And after we[re] polluted slepynge? Hast þow do þat synne bale 1384 By any wommon þat lay in hale?
Hast thou tried to seduce any woman,	Hast þow wowet[1] any wyghte, And tempted hyre ouer nyghte? Hast þou made þe gay þerfore, 1388 Þat heo schulde þe loue þe more? Hast þou desyred syche to be, Þat wymmen schulde loue þe?
or taken delight in lustful songs?	Hast þou hade lykynge for to here 1392 Songes þat of lechery were?

[1] wowed.

CONCERNING VENIAL SINS. 43

Hast þou cou*n*selet or do socowre
By any wey to a lechowre?
Be-þenke þe, sone, in vche degre
1396 What in þy thoghte be-fel þe;
Ȝef þow conne any þynge mynne,[1]
Þat perteneth to þat synne.

Hast thou aided any one in such wicked courses?

Quod si sit femina.

¶ And ȝef heo be a wo*m*mon,
1400 Byd hyre telle, ȝef heo con,
Of what degre þe mon was
That synned wyþ hyre in þe cas,
Syb or sengul or any spowse,
1404 Or what degre of relygyowse,
Or wheþer hyt were a-gayn hyre wylle,
Or wheþer heo a-sented fully þer-tylle,
Or wheþer hyt were for couetyse
1408 Of gold or selu*er* or oght of hyse,
Þenne þe synne dowbul were,
And neded penawnce myche more.
Why & where, how & whenne,
1412 And how ofte aske hyre þenne,
Of alle poyntes þow moste wyte,
As by-fore I haue wryte.

If it be a woman bid her tell thee of what degree the man was that sinned with her; whether he was single or wedded, or a religious,

and whether she were ravished or consented thereto,

and whether she did it for pay, for then the sin double were.

¶ *De modo inquirendi de peccatis venialibus.*

1416 Now of synnes venyal,
A luyte[2] aske þe I schal:
Hast þow spende þy wytt*us* fyue
To godd*us* worschype? telle me blyue.
Þese ben þey as I þe telle,
1420 Towche & tast & eke þy smelle,
Þy herynge also and þy syȝt,
Here þey be fyue on ryȝt.

Of venial sins.

Hast thou spent thy wits in God's [Fol. 144.] service?

---

[1] nyme.   [2] litul.

¶ De risu.

¶ Hast þow I-seyn any thynge
1424 þat tysed þe to synnynge?
Be-þenke þe, sone, welle I pray
For mony þyngus þat falle may.

¶ De auditu.

¶ Hast þow I-had gret lykynge
1428 For to here euele thynge,
Or nyce wordes of rybawdy,
Or suche maner harlotry?

¶ De olfactu.

¶ Hast þow I-smelled any þynge
1432 þat hath tend thy lykynge,
Of mete or drynke or spysory
þat þow hast after I-synned by?

¶ De gustu.

¶ Also ȝef þou synned hast,
1436 In mete or drynke by lusty tast,
þat also þow moste telle me,
ȝef I schale a-soyle the.

¶ De tactu.

¶ Hast þou I-towched folyly,
1440 þat þy membrus were styred by,
Wommones flesch or þyn owne?
ȝef þow hast þou moste schowne.
Here ben þe wyttus fyue,
1444 How þey ben spende telle me blyue,
And whad þou hast in herte more,
Telle me, sone, a-non by-fore
I praye þe, sone, be not a-ferd,
1448 But telle hyt owte now a-pert.
Telle me, sone, I the pray,

I wolc þe helpe ȝof þat I may.

¶ Is þy penaunce alle I-do,   *Hast thou done all thy penances?*
1452 Þat þy schryffader ioynet þe to?
For-gyuest þow wyth herte fre,   *Dost thou forgive all that have trespassed against thee?*
Alle þo þat haue trespaset to þe?
Any vow hast þow I-mad?   *Hast thou kept all vows that thou hast made?*
1456 Hast þou þat holden ferme and sad?
Hast þow eten any sonday   [Fol. 144 back.]
    Hast thou eaten on Sundays without holy bread?
Wíth-owte halybred? say ȝe or nay.
Hast þou I-storbet prest or clerk   *Hast thou disturbed priest or clerk at his work?*
1460 Þat were bysy in goddes werk?
Hast þou I-had or wyst where,
Þat was I-asked in chyrche þere?
Hast þow wyþowte knowlachynge   *Hast thou wished thyself accursed?*
1464 I-wyst þe a-corsed for any þynge?
Art þow I-wont at lychwake   *Art thou wont to make plays at any likewake?*
Any pleyes for to make?
Þe werkes of mercy summe & alle   *Hast thou done works of mercy?*
1468 Hast þou I-wroȝt as þe by-felle?

¶ Hast þow holpe by þy myȝt   *Hast thou helped to bury the dead?*
To burye þe dede as byd owre dryȝt?
Pore & naked and hongry,   *Hast thou succoured the poor?*
1472 Hast þow I-sokeret mekely?
Hast þou in herte rowþe I-had,   *Hast thou done kindly deeds to the sick prisoners and wayfarers.*
Of hem þat were nede be-stad,
To seke & sore and prisonerus,
1476 I-herberet alle weyferus?
Hast þou I-lyued also in chost & stryf   *Hast thou quarrelled with thy wife?*
Wyþ þy meyne and wyþ þy wyf?
Hast þow also by hyre I-layn,   *Have thou and she overlain any of your infants?*
1480 And so by-twene ȝow þe chylde I-slayn?
Also þy chyldre þat were schrewes,   *Hast thou kept thy children in subjection?*
Hast þow I-taght hem gode þewes?
Hast þow ouer-holde corne or ote,[1]   *Hast thou overheld corn?*
1484 Or oþer þynge þat come neuer to note?

    [1] wote.

Hast thou frequented the company of cursed men, to succour them, or to preach to them for their good?

For to lene hast þow be loth,
And for to quite hast þou be wroth?
¶ Hast þow be in corset cumpany,
1488 Of corset men? telle me why,
To socour hem wyþ bodyly fode,
Or to preche hem for here gode?
Who so sokereth hem in here malys,
1492 He ys as corsed as þey I-wys.

Hast thou hindered matrimony?
[Fol. 145.]

Telle also for the bet
Matrymony ȝef þow haue let.

*Hast thou passed by a churchyard and neglected to pray for the dead?
Hast thou ever left open a gate so that beasts have gone in?
Hast thou destroyed corn, grain, or other things that were sown?*

Hast þow I-come by chyrche ȝorde,
1496 And for þe dede I-prayed no worde?
Hast þow ay cast vp lyde ȝate
Þere bestus haue go in ate?
Hast þow I-struyed corn or gras,
1500 Or oþer þynge þat sowen was?
Hast þou I-come in any sty
And cropped ȝerus of corne¹ þe by?

Art thou wont to ride over corn.

Art þou I-wont ouer corn to ryde
1504 When þou myȝtest haue go by syde?
Ȝef þow haue more in herte,
Telle me, sone, now alle smerte;
For alle þat þow helest now fro me
1508 Þe fende fulle redyly wole telle þe.
But when he con no more sayn,
Þen ȝeue hym penaunce withowte layn.

¶ *De modo iniungendi penitenciam.*

Of the manner of enjoining penance.

1512 Now confessour I warne þe,
Here connynge þow moste be,
Wayte þat þow be slegh & fel
To vnderstonde hys schryft wel;
Wherfore þese þynges þow moste wyte
1516 That in þys vers nexte be wryte.

¹ MS. corner.

¶ *Quis, quid, vbi, per quos, quociens, quomodo, quando.*

¶ Fyrst þow moste þys mynne,[1] You must bear in mind who the penitent is;
What he ys þat doth þe synne,
Wheþer hyt be heo or he, whether young or old, bond or free, poor or rich,
1520 ȝonge or olde, bonde or fre,
Pore or ryche, or in offys,
Or mon of dyguyte ȝef he ys,
Sengul or weddet or cloystrere, single or married, clerk or secular person,
1524 Clerke, or lewed, or seculere,
Byschope or prest, or mon of state,
Þow moste wyte þese al gate.
Þe herre þat a mon ys in degre,
1528 Þe sarrer forsoþe falleþ he,
And ȝef he were in hys wyt, and whether he be in his wits or no.
Also þow moste wyte hyt.
What synne hyt ys and how I-wroȝt,
1532 To wyte redyly spare þow noght, [Fol. 145 back.] You must be heedful to know all his sin,
Wheþer hyt be gret or smal,
Opan or hud wyte þow al.
Lechery, robbery, or monslaȝt,
1536 Byd hym telle euen straȝt.
For summe telleþ not here synne al, for some will not tell all their sin.
In confessyone general.
Þus a mon may other whyle
1540 Þe and hym boþe by-gyle.
Hyt ys to luyte for any mon It is not sufficient for the penitent to say he has slain a man; he must say who he was, wherefore, and why.
To say he hath slayn a mon.
But ȝef he telle hyt openly,
1544 What mon he was, wharfore, & why,
Wheþer hyt be fader or broþer,
Prest or clerke, or any other.
Also men sayn comynly A man who has sinned in lechery must not mention
1548 I haue synned in lechery,

[1] nyme.

the name of the other person unless it be needful.	ȝet most þow wyte by whom hyt ys, Or elles ȝe mowe do boþe a-mys. But nome he schal non telle þe;
	1552 But ȝef þe synne syche be, þat he ne may hys schryfte telle, But he take hyre in hys spelle, þen he may þe name mynge.
	1556 Ellus hym aȝte for no þynge;
But he must tell in what state and condition of life she was,	But wheþer ho be wyf or may, Syb or fremde, make hym say, Nonne or ankeras, or what degre,
	1560 Algate make hym telle the; For ȝef þe synne be gret or grym, þe more penaunce nedeth hym;
and whether or not the sin was done in a holy place,	Were hyt was wyte þou also
	1564 In holy place or no. A mon synneþ sarre in seyntwary þenne in any oþer place by, By whom also þow moste mynne,
	1568 And whom he gart to do þat synne, And whad þey were þat were here ferus, Prestes or clerkus, monkes or frerus, þe mo to synne that he droghe,
[Fol. 146.]	1572 Þe more for-sothe hym-self he sloghe; How ofte also he dyde that dede,
and how often the sin was done, for the oftener it is done the more the sin is.	Wyte at hym þow moste nede, For euer so ofter newed hyt ys,
	1576 Þe gratter þe synne waxeth I-wys; So ofter a wounde ys I-cot þe worse to hele hyt nede be mot; þe ofter a mon doth monslaghte,
	1580 Þe more he ys the fende by-taghte; þe ofter he doth lechery, þe ofter he synneth dedly; Dedly he synneth wyþowte drede,
	1584 As ofte as he þat synne doþ brede,

And why he dyde þat ylke synne,
Also nede he mote mynne:
Wheþer hyt were for loue or drede,
1588 Or couetyse of worldes mede,
Or for enuye, or for debate,
Or for wrathþe of olde hate,
And he dyde he mote say,
1592 And not hele hyt by no way.
Wheþer he dyde þat in hastynes,
Or wel a-vyset ȝef he wes;
For he þat casteth hym to do a dede,
1596 More penaunce he mote haue nede
Þen he þat doth hyt sodenlycho,
And afterward hym reweth myche;
And whenne hyt was and what day,
1600 Byd hym to the that he say,
For on a halyday ȝef he synne,
Nedely to þe he mote hyt mynne,
Or any oþer fastynge day,
1604 Lentun or vygyle, as telle he may,
For gratter synne for soþe hyt ys
On suche dayes to do a-mys,
Myche more wythoute nay,
1608 Þen on a-noþer werkeday,
And ȝet more by-fore none
Þen afterward and hyt were done,
Þerfore þou moste wel hyt mynne,
1612 Boþe tyde & tyme, he þat doth synne.
Alle þese poyntus þow moste wyte,
Þat here be-fore ben I-wryte;
Or elles gode dome þou myȝt not ȝeue
1616 Of men þat beth to the I-schryue,
So þow myȝt knowe sum and al,
Wheþer þe synne be gret or smal,
And ȝef þe synne be fowle & grym,
1620 The gratter penaunce ȝeue þou hym;

He must also say whether he sinned for love or fear.

He must say on what day he sinned, for a sin done on a holy day or fasting day is worse than one committed at another time.

[Fol. 146 back.]

All these things must be known, or else the confessor cannot give a good dome.

If the sin be great, so must the penance be.

If the sin be light, let the penance be light also.	And ȝef þe synne be but luyte, To þe lasse penaunce þou hym putte; But fyrst take hede by gode a-vys,
	1624 Of what contrycyone þat he ys,
If the man is sorry for his sin, let the penance be abridged;	ȝef he be sory for hys synne, And fulle contryte as þou myȝt kenne; Wepeþ faste and ys sory,
	1628 And asketh ȝerne of mercy, A-bregge hys penaunce þen by myche, For god hym self for-ȝeueth syche;
but if he be stiff of heart the penance must be heavy,	ȝef he be styf & of herte heȝ,
	1632 Grope hym softe & go hym neȝ, And when þou herest where he wole byde, ȝeue hym penaunce þenne also þat tyde,
but still such as he will perform;	But non oþer þen he wole take
	1636 Wors þenne lest þow hym make. Take gode hede on hys de-gre Of what skynnes¹ lyuyuge þat he be,
[Fol. 147.]	For on may soffre þat a-noþer ne may,
	1640 Þerfore set hym in syche way, Þat hys penaunce he may do ryȝt, Be hyt heuy, be hyt lyȝt;
for if a man has more laid on him than he will do, he will cast it all aside and be worse than if he had not gone to confession.	ȝef þow ley on hym more
	1644 Þenne he wole asente fore, Alle he wole caste hym fro, And schende hym-self, I telle þe so, Wharfore be wys and war,
	1648 For mony men fulle dyuers ar. Now take hede what I þe mynne, ȝef a wyf haue done a synne,
A woman's penance must be such as her husband may not know.	Syche penaunce þou gyue hyre þenne
	1652 Þat hyre husbonde may not kenne, Leste for þe penaunce sake Wo & w[r]aþþe by-twene hem wake.

¹ kynnes.

Wharfore þe nedeth to be wys,
1656 For, forsothe, gret nede hyt ys,
Lest þow do oȝt on madhede,
And sende so al to þe quede;
Bettur hyt ys wyth penaunce lutte, — *Better with a light penaunce to send a man to purgatory, than with penaunce overmuch to send him to hell.*
1660 In-to purgatory a mon to putte,
Þen wyþ penaunce ouer myche,
Sende hym to helle putte.[1]
Wharfore lerne þys lessoun wel,
1664 And take gode hede to my spel,
Countur wyþ countur ys I-huled ofte,
When þey be leyde to-gedur softe.

¶ Contra superbiam.

Agaynus pruyde wythowte les, — *Pride. The remedy for it is meekness.*
1668 Þe forme remedy ys mekenes,
Ofte to knele and erþe to kys, — *It is good for thee to kiss the earth and look on dead men's bones, and think on the pains of hell and Christ's passion.*
And knowlache wel þat erþe he ys,
And dede mennus bonus ofte to se,
1672 And þenke þat he schal syche be.
Þe peynes of helle haue ȝerne in thoȝt,
And domes day for-ȝete thow noght,
Crystus passyone haue in mynde,
1676 Þat sleth pruyde, as wryten I fynde,
And who so þenketh þus in stedefast thoȝt,[2]
Pruyde he schale sette at noȝt.

¶ Contra Iram.[3]

Agaynes wraþþe hys helpe schal be, — *Wrath. Against this sin the remedy is for a man to see how angels flee from him when he is angry, and fiends fast to him run and burn his heart with hell-fire;*
1680 Ȝef he haue grace in herte to se
How aungelus, when he ys wroth,
From hym faste flen and goth,
And fendes faste to hym renneth,
1684 And wyþ fuȝre of helle hys herte breneth,

---

[1] pitche. [2] The above four lines are not in Douce 103. [3] MS. *Iiram.*

And maketh hym so hote & hegh,
þat no mon may byde hym negh,
And makeþ hym syche as þey arn

and make him such as they are —of God's child the devil's bairn.

1688 Of goddes chylde þe doueles barn,
Wharfore he mote wyth sofferynge,
Quenche in hym syche brennynge,
A-gaynus wrathþe soferaunce
1692 Mote be myche hys penaunce.

¶ *Contra Inuidiam.*

Envy.

A Gayn enuye loue ys gryth,
But ȝet he mote do more wyth,
Serues to hym wyth herte fre
1696 To whom he hath enuyes I-be.
Louynge serues and godely speche
Agayn enuye ys helpe and leche.

¶ *Contra auariciam.*

Covetousness.

D O also in thys wyse
1700 I bydde a-ȝeynes couetyse,
Quyte a-gayn a-byde not to longe,
þat þow hast take wyth wronge,
And to þe nedy ȝeue þow large,
1704 In goddus name I þe charge.

¶ *Contra gulam.*

Gluttony.

O F þy fowle gloterye
Abstene þe, I bydde þe hye,
And for þy lust & þy sorfet
1708 þow moste do almes fulle gret;
Fede þe pore of þat þow sparest,
And lete hem fele how þow farest.

¶ *Contra accidiam.*

[Fol. 148.]
Sloth.
The remedy is to say the pater noster at morn, midday, and eventide;

¶ Slowthe þow moste to gode turne,
1712 And þy pater noster say ȝerne,
In morowe & mydday & euentyde,
Wheþer þow go oþer þow ryde

  To chyrche come ȝef þow may,
1716 And here þy masse vche day,   *to hear mass each day, and if work hinders from going to church, to join in heart in the service when the mass knell is heard.*
  And ȝef þow may not come to chyrche,
  Where euer þat þow do worche,
  When þow herest to masse knylle,
1720 Prey to god wyþ herte stylle,
  To ȝeue þe part of þat seruyse,
  Þat in chyrche I-done ys.

  ¶ *Contra luxuriam.*

  Thagh þow þenke þy lechery swete,   *echery.*
1724 Lef þow hyt I the hete,
  And lerne to lyue in chastyte,
  In goddes name I charge þe;
  And for þy flesch þer-in has game,
1728 Wíth bred & water þou schalt hyt tame,   *Tame the flesh by bread and water.*
  And ȝef he say a-gayn to þe,
  He may not lyue in chastyte,
  Charge hym þenne to take a wyf,   *He who cannot live in chastity to take a wife.*
1732 In goddes lawe to lede hys lyf,
  And þaȝ he say he wole not do so,
  Ȝet penaunce make hym to do;
  Hyt schale do gode here or henne,
1736 Laske hys peynes or cese hys synne.

  ¶ *Quanta sit penitencia pro mortalibus.*

  On dedly synne, as lawes techeth,   *The legal penance for mortal sin.*
  To seuen ȝerus ende recheth,
  Faste bred & water vche fryday,
1740 And for-go flesch on wednesday,
  The same dayes þorȝ þe ȝere,
  That schal laste fully souen ȝere;
  But now be fewe þat wole do so,   *There are now few who will perform it.*
1744 Þerfore a lyȝter way þou moste go;
  A monnes contricyone be-holde þou ȝerne,
  Þer-by þy domes thow moste lerne;

          Ȝef hyt be gret ȝeue luyte penaunce,
1748 Ȝef hyt be luyte þow moste hyt vaunce,[1]
          Be hyt more, be hyt lasse,
          After þe contricyone þe dome moste passe.
          Be not to harde I þe rede,
1752 But ay do mercy in goddes drede,
          He ys ful of me[r]cy ay,
          Be þou also I the pray,
          For lasse synnes venyal,
1756 Lasse penaunce ȝeue þow schal,
          So þat þe synne hys herte greue,
          And be in purpos hyt to leue,
          I hope here be I-noȝ I-wryte,
1760 To teche a prest how he schale wyte,
          To ȝeue a dome of monnes synne
          Ȝef any wyt be hym wyþynne.

¶ *Isti mittendi sunt ad episcopum.*

          Bvt confessour be wys and ȝop,
1764   And sende forth þese to þe byschop:
          Alle þat smyteþ prest or clerk,
          And hem þat worcheþ wycked werk,
          Hows brenner & sleer of mon,
1768 And fader or modur in vyolens þat leyþ hond vp-on,
          Þe modur þat þe chylde ouer lyth,
          Þe fader also sende þow wyth,
          A mon þat ys a-corset wyþ book & belle,
1772 And eretykes as I the telle;
          Hym þat brekeþ solempne vow,
          Or chawnge hyt wole, sende hym forþ now;
          Clypper of þe kynges mynt,
1776 And hym þat lyueth by swerdes dynt
          Alle fals sysourus and okererus,
          And hem þat fals wytnes berus;

---

[1] haunce.

ABSOLUTION.

Alle þat be wedded vnlawfully,
1780 Or susterus or cosynus lyggeþ by;
And alle þo, schortely to say,
þat þe grete sentens a-corseþ ay;
And ȝef þe byschope a-corse mo,
1784 Sende hem forth-wyth also.

those who have lain with sisters or cousins; and all that are cursed by the great excommunication.

[Fol. 149.]

¶ *De modo absoluendi penitentem.*

Now take hede how þow schalt done
Of thyn absolucyone;
When schryfte ys herde þen ȝeue penaunce,
1788 And bydde hym say wyth fulle creawnce:

Absolution: how it is given.

¶ *Et dicat confitens.*

"God, I crye þe mercy,
And þy moder seynt mary,
And alle þe seyntus of heuen bryȝt,
1792 I crye mercy wyth alle my myȝt,
Of alle þe synnus I haue wroȝt,
In werke and worde, & sory þoȝt,
Wyth euery lyme of my body,
1796 Wyth sore herte I aske god mercy,
And þe, fader, in goddes place,
A-soyle me þow of my trespace,
Ȝeue me penaunce also to,
1800 For goddes loue þat þow so do."

A form of confession.

¶ *Tunc dicat sacerdos.*

Ego auctoritate dei patris omnipotentis & [beatorum¹] apostolorum petri & pauli & officij michi commissi in hac parte absoluo te ab hijs peccatis michi
1804 per te confessis & ab alijs de quibus non recordaris.
In nomine patris & filij & spiritus sancti. Amen.
Ista humilitas & passio domini nostri ihesu christi

The form of absolution.

---

¹ Not in Douce 103.

& merita sancte matris ecclesie & omnes indulgencie
1808 tibi concesse & omnia bona que fecisti & facies vsque
in finem vite tue sint tibi in remissionem istorum &
omnium aliorum peccatorum tuorum. Amen.

Extreme unction

¶ *De sacramento extreme vnccionis.*

 Hyt ys not gode to be helut,
1812 How a wyȝt schal be an-elet,

to be given when a man is near death.

When þat he ys so ouer-dryue,
þat he may no lengur lyue,
þenne he schale an-elet be,
1816 And non er, I warne the,
But þaȝ he be an-elet ones,
ȝet he may eftsones,
But he þat ys in hys wyt,

He who despises this sacrament will be damned.

1820 And be so temptut despyseþ hyt,
Haue he in herte non oþer mynne,
He schale be dampned for þat synne,
But he þat schale be an-oynt,

[Fol. 149 back.]

1824 Aske hym þus euery poynt:

Infirmus dicta ȝe.

Questions to be asked of the sick person.
Dost thou die in the Christian faith?

¶ "Art þow fayn, my broþer, say,
þat þow dyest in crysten fay?
Myȝt þou also in þy herte se

Has thy life been worse than it should be?

1828 þat þy lyf ys worse þen hyt scholde be? ȝe.
For-þynkeþ þe, telle me þys,

Hast thou lived amiss?
Hast thou a will to amend if thy life be spared?

þat þou hast lad þy lyf a-mys? ȝe.
Hast þow wyl þe to a-mende,
1832 ȝef god wole þe lyf sende? ȝe.

Believest thou on the Lord's passion?

Be-leuest þow with ful gode deuocyone
On ihesu crystes passyone? ȝe.

And how it alone can save thee?

And how hys passyone saue þe schal,
1836 And by non oþer way at al? ȝe.

Hold up both hands and thank Christ, and pray

Holde vp now boþe þy hondes
And þonke criste of alle hys sondes,

And praye hym, for hys moder sake, *him for his mother's sake that he will take thy soul.*
1840 þat he wole þy sowle take
In-to hys honde and hys kepynge,
And saue hyt from þe fowle þynge.
ȝef he con þys oresone say,
1844 Byd hym say hyt wyþowte delay.

¶ *Oracio dicenda ab infirmo ante vnccionem.*

Deus meus, deus meus, misericordia mea & refugium *Prayer to be said by the sick man.*
meum, te desidero, ad te confugio, ad te festino
venire. ne despicias me sub tremendo discrimine
1848 positum; adesto michi propicius in hijs magnis meis
necessitatibus: non possum me redimere meis opera-
cionibus. Sed tu, deus meus, redime me & miserere
mei. diffido de meis meritis, sed magis confido de misera-
1852 cionibus tuis & plus confido de miseracionibus tuis quam
diffido de malis meis actibus. tu spes mea, deus meus,
tibi soli peccaui; mea culpa, mea maxima culpa. nunc
ad te venio quia nulli deos; cupio dissolui & esse tecum.
1856 In manus tuas domine commendo spiritum meum, re-
demisti me domine deus veritatis. Amen. Et patra
michi deus meus, vt in pace dormiam & requiescam.
Qui in trinitate perfecta viuis & regnas deus per
1860 omnia¹ secula seculorum. Amen.

¶ *Tunc vngatur infirmus.*

ȝEt I wole wryte more, *Further instructions to men of mean lore.*
 To hym þat ys mene of lore,
Of neclygens, more & lasse, *Of negligence that may befal in the mass.*
1864 þat may be-falle in þe masse.
Fyrst se, prest, as I þe mynne, *A priest who says mass must be out of deadly sin.*
þat þow be out of dedly synne, [Fol. 150.]
Þyn auter þenne þou do dyȝt,
1868 þat hyt be after thy myȝt.

¹ infinita.

The altar cloths must be clean, and all of them hallowed. Three towels to be on the altar at mass.	Se þe cloþes þat þey be clene, And also halowet alle by-dene, Wyth þre towayles and no lasse 1872 Hule þyn auter at thy masse, Al oþer thynge þow knowest wel, What þe nedeth euer-y del.
The candle to be of wax,	Loke þat þy candel of wax hyt be, 1876 And set hyre, so þat þow hyre se, On þe lyfte half of þyn autere,
and to burn clearly.	And loke algate ho brenne clere, Wayte þat ho brenne in alle wyse, 1880 Tyl þow haue do þat seruyse.
The bread to be of wheaten flour.	Þy bred schal be of whete flour, I-made of dogh that ys not sour, Þat hyt be rounde and hol wayte wel,
The wine not sour. Water to be put to the wine.	1884 And loke þy wyn be not eysel; Poure water to thy wyn, As þow const wel and fyn, Sey þe wordes of þat seruyse
The tails of the words not to be cut.	1888 Deuowtely wyth gode a-vyse; Cotte þow not þe wordes tayle, But sey hem oute wyþowte fayle; Sey hem so wyþ mowþe & thoght
	1892 Þat oþer þynge þow þenke noght, But al þyn herte & þyn entent Be fully on that sacrament.
If it happen, through accident, that bread or wine be not on the altar when mass is being said, lay bread on the corporax, and begin again at "qui pridie."	Ȝef hyt be-falle, as god hyt scylde, 1896 Þat þow of wyt be so wylde, Þat bred or wyn be a-way, Consecracyone when þou scholdest say; Ȝef þe be-falle þat ylke cas, 1900 Ley bred on þy corporas, And þaȝ þow forth I-passet be, Be-gynne a-gayn "qui pridie."
[Fol. 150 back.] If wine and water are absent,	Ȝef wyn and water be bothe a-way, 1904 Powre in boþe wythowte lay,

And tur̄ne a-gayn as I þe kenne,
And " simili modo" say þow þenne.
ȝef þou haue water and no wyn,
1908 A-non-ryȝt do hyt yn,
And by-gynne, as I ȝer taȝte,
At " simili modo" euen straȝte ;
And ȝef þow be neȝ þe ende,
1912 ȝef syche mynde god þe sende,
Þat þow haue wyn & no water,
Þen powre hyt in neuer þe later,
And by-gynne "oremus,
1916 Preceptis salutaribus."
ȝef þe wonte stole or fanoun,
When þow art in þe canoun,
Passe forth wythowten turne,
1920 But þat þow moste rewe ȝerne ;
ȝef a drope of blod by any cas
Falle vp-on þe corporas,
Sowke hyt vp a-non-ryȝt,
1924 And be as sory as þou myȝt,
Þe corporas after þow folde,
A-monge þe relekus to be holde ;
On oþer þynge ȝef hyt falle,
1928 On vestement oþer on palle,
A-wey þow moste þe pece cotte,
And hyt brenne & a-monge þe relekus putte ;
ȝef hyt falle on sum oþer what,
1932 Tabul or ston, vrþe or mat,
Lyk hyt vp clene þat ys sched,
And schaf hyt after þat ys be-bled,
And do þe schauynge for to brenne,
1936 Amonge þe relekus put hyt þenne ;
ȝef any flye, gnat, or coppe
Doun in-to þe chalys droppe,
ȝef þow darst for castynge þere,
1940 Vse hyt hol alle I-fere,

supply them, and begin at "simili modo."

If you have water and no wine, supply it, and begin again at the same place.

If you have forgotten stole or fannon go forth for them.

If a drop of blood fall on the corporax, suck it up, and be as sorry as you can for it, and put the corporax away among the relics.

If it fall on anything else, lick it up and shave the place, and burn the shavings and put the ashes among the relics.

If a gnat, fly, or spider fall into the cup, swallow it.

[Fol. 151.]

If you are afraid of vomiting, take it out with your hand and wash it over the chalice and then burn it.	And ȝef þy herte do wyþstonde, Take vp the fulþe wyþ þyn honde, And ouer the chalys wosche hyt wel

    1944 Twyes or thryes, as I þe telle,
            And vse forth þe blod þenne,
            And do þe fulþe for to brenne;
            Do more ȝet also thow most,

Change the host each day.
    1948 Vche day chawnge þyn ost,
            Redy þat þow haue mowe,
            To vche seke ay I-nowe.

¶ *Ad huc alia necessaria capellano scire.*

            } Et lerne þys for thy prow,
    1952 { þat I wryte after now.

Go fast to the sick.
            When þow schalt to seke gon,
            Hye þe faste & go a-non;
            For ȝef þow tarye þow dost a-mys,
    1956 þow schalt quyte that sowle I-wys;

When thou goest put on a clean surplice, take thy stole with thee, and pull thy hood over thy eyes.
            When þow schalt to seke gon,
            A clene surples caste þe on,
            Take þy stole wyth þe ryȝt,
    1960 And pul thy hod ouer þy syȝt,

Bear the host on thy breast.
            Bere þyn ost a-nont þy breste,
            In a box that ys honeste.

Cause the clerk to bear a light and ring a bell before thee.
            Make þy clerk be-fore þe ȝynge,
    1964 To bere lyȝt and belle rynge,
            On þy power þen haue þow mynne,
            þat þow myȝt a-soyle of alle synne;

In peril of death thou hast the power to assoil from all sin.
            In perel of deth þow hast powere
    1968 Of alle synne to a-soyle clere;
            But ȝef þe seke turne to lyue,
            Of þat same synne he mote hym schryue,
            And hys penaunce take newe,
    1972 For alle þynge þat he er schewe,

Spare not to ask the sick of his sins [Fol. 151 back.]
            And spare þow not for no let
            To aske hym of hys det,

And whether hyt be myche or luyte,
1976 Charge hym þat he hyt quyte,
And ȝef hys godes to luyte be
For to quyte þat oweth he,
Charge hym þenne wyth herte lowe
1980 To aske mercy of þat he owe;
And ȝet þow moste lerne þys eke,
Of a mon þat ys ful seke,
Þat sendeþ to þe to hym to ryde,
1984 And waxe dowmbe in þat tyde,
Ȝef he by synes þat hosul soghte,
Thaȝ þow knowe þow schryue hym noȝte,
Nerþeles þow schalt hym soyle,
1988 And ȝeue hym hosul & holy oyle.
When þou hast þe seke I-schryue,
And þow se þat he may not lyue,
Oþer penaunce þow schalt not gyn
1992 But þe sekenes þat he ys In,
Ioyne þat sekenes & þat sore
By-fore god to be hys ore;
And ȝef he aske hys sauyour,
1996 Gyf hym hyt wyþ gret honour;
But ȝef he be so seke wyth-ynne
Þat of castynge he may not blynne,
He schal not þenne hys hosul take,
2000 For vomyschment & castynge sake,
But preche hym feyre wyth opun spelle
Þat god a-loweth hys herte & hys wylle,
And for he wolde & he myȝte,
2004 God hym takeþ in hys ryȝto.
Ȝet when þou art to chyrche I-went,
Do vp so that sacrament
Þat hyt be syker in vche way,
2008 Þat no best hyt towche may.
Ȝef hyt [were] eten wyth mows or rat,
Dere þow moste a-bygge þat;

Charge him with lowly heart to ask mercy.

If a sick man cannot speak, but by signs shews that he wishes for the housel and holy oil, they are to be given to him.

The sick person to have no other penance given but his sickness.

If he is so sick that he would vomit up the holy eucharist, it is not to be given to him, but he is to be told that the desire for it is sufficient.

The host to be made secure in church, so that no mouse or rat may eat it.

[Fol. 152.]

	Fowrty dayes for þat myschawnce
	2012 þow schalt be in penau*n*ce.
If any crumb of it be lost it must be sought for.	ȝef any crome of hyt be lost,
	ȝerne seche hyt þow most,
	ȝef þow hyt fynde no wey myȝte,
	2016 þrytty dayes þow rewe hyt ryȝte;
If through malice thou singest mass without water and a light, thou must do penance till the bishop restore thee.	And ȝef þow be so vnwys
	þat þow synge by malys,
	Wythowte wat*er* and lyȝt also,
	2020 And wost well*e* þe wonteth bo,
	þow schalt þenne for þy song*e*
	Boþe wepe and weyle er a-mong*e*,
	Tyl þe hyschope of hys ore
	2024 To þy song*e* the restore.
	¶ *Oracio opificis opusculi h*u*ius.*
The priest to pray for the author,	Now, dere prest, I pray þe,
	For goddes loue þow pray for me,
	More I pray þat þow mo mynge,
and to remember him when he sings mass.	2028 In þy masse when thow dost synge;
	And ȝet I pray þe, leue broþer,
	Rede þys ofte, and so lete oþ*er*,
	Huyde hyt not in hodymoke,
	2032 Lete other mo rede þys boke;
	The mo þer-In doth rede & lerne,
	þe mo to mede hyt schal*e* torne;
This book is made to instruct those who have no books of their own, and others of mean lore.	Hyt ys I-made hem to schowne
	2036 þat haue no bokes of here owne,
	And oþ*er* þat beth of mene lore,
	þat wolde fayn conne more,
	And þow þat here-In lernest most,
	2040 Thonke ȝerne þe holy gost,
[Fol. 152 back.]	That ȝeueþ wyt to vche mon
	To do þe gode that he con,
	And by hys t*r*auayle and hys ded*e*
	2044 ȝcueþ hym heuen to hys mede;

The mede and þe ioye of heuen lyȝt
God vs graunte For hys myght. Amen.

Explicit tractatus qui dicitur pars oculi de latino in anglicum translatus per fratrem Iohannem myrcus canonicum regularem Monasterij de Lylleshul, cuius anime propicietur deus. Amen.

LANSDOWNE MS. 762, Fol. 21b.

Here folowethe vij specialle interrogacions The whiche a Curat aught to aske euery cristene persone that liethe in the extremytie of dethe.

The first. Belevest thowe fully alle the pryncipalle articles of the Feithe and also alle holy scripturs in alle thyngis after the exposicione of the holy & trewe doctours of holy Chirche & forsakest alle heresies & arrours & opynyons dampned by the Chirche. and arte glad also that thowe shalt dye in the feithe of Criste & in the vnytie & obedience of holy Chirche? The Sike persone answerethe, Yee. *Dost thou beleve the principal articles of the faith and the holy Scriptures, and dost thou forsake heresy?*

The second. knowest thowe & knowligest thowe nowe thowe oftene tymes & many maner wise & grevowsely thowe hast offended thy lorde god that made the of nought, for saint Barnard saithe vpon Canticac anticorum, I knowe wele that there maye no manne be saved but yef he knowe hym self. Of the whiche knowlage wexethe a manne the Moder of his helthe that is humylitie, and also the drede of God, the whiche drede, as it is the begynnyng of wisdome, So it is the begynnyng of mannys Soule? he answerethe, Yee. *Dost thou know that thou hast often offended God?*

The thirde. Arte thowe sory in thy harte of alle maner of Synnys that thowe hast doone ayenst the highe Magestie and the love and the goodnesse of God & of alle goodnesse *Art thou sorry for thy sins?*

that thowe hast not & myghtyst haue doone & of alle graces that thowe hast forslowthed, not onely for drede of dethe [*Fol. 22a.] *or any other payne, but rather more for love of god & rightvsnesse & for thowe hast displeased his grete goodnesse & kyndenesse & for the due ordre & charitie by the whiche we be boundene to love god aboue alle thynge & of alle thise thynges thowe askest forgevenes of god? desirest thowe also in thyne harte to haue very knowing of alle the offences that thowe hast doone ayenst god, and for to haue specialle repentaunce of theym alle? he answerethe, Yee.

and desirest to amend?

The Fourthe. Purposest thowe verely & arte in fulle wille to amende the & thowe myghtest live lenger & neuer to Synne more dedely wittyngly & with thy wille, & Rather thanne thowe woldest offende god dedely any more, to leve & lese wilfully alle erthly thynges, were they neuer so lefe to the, and also the life of thy body, and farthermore thowe prayest God, that he yeve the grace to contynue in this purpose? he answerethe, Yee.

Dost thou forgive thy enemies?

The Fifte. Foryevest thowe fully in thy harte alle maner of menne that euer hauet he any harme or grevaunce vnto this tyme other in worde or in dede for the love & the worshipe of our lorde Ihesu criste to whome thowe hopest to haue forgivenesse of thy selfe, & askest also thy self to haue forgivenesse of alle theym that thowe hast offended in any maner wise? he answerethe, Yee.

Art thou willing in all manner to make satisfaction?

The Sixte. Wolde thowe that alle maner thynges that thowe hast in any maner wise myght be fully restored ayeyne as moche as thowe mayest & thowe arte bounde after the value of thy good & rather leve & forsake alle thy good of the worlde yef thowe mayest not make satisfaccione in none other wise? he answerethe, Yee.

Dost thou believe that Christ died for thee? [*Fol. 22b.]

The Seventhe. Belevest thowe fully that Criste dyed *for the, and that thowe may neuer be saved but by the Merite of Cristes passione, and thanne thankest therof god with thyne harte asmoche as thowe mayest? he answerethe, Yee.

ASKED OF ONE NEAR DEATH. 65

Than*n*e let the Curat desire the sike p*erso*n*e* to saye In Manus tuas & *cetera* with*e* a good stedfast mynde and yf that he can*n*e, And yef he cannot let the Curat saye it for hym, And who so cu*er* may verely of very good consience & trowth*e* w*it*hout any faynyng answere, yee, to all*e* the articles & poynt*es* afore Rehersed, he shall*e* live eu*er* in hevyn*e* w*ith* all*e* myghtie god and with*e* his holy Cvmpany, whervnto Ih*es*us brynge both*e* yowe and me.   Amo*n*e.

<small>The curate to cause the sick person to say "in manus tuas." If he cannot say it the curate is to say it for him.</small>

NOTES.

Page 1, line 5. *Dawe*, plural of Day. A.S. *Dæg*,

" Wel is us nu, Louerd, uor þe *dawes* þet tu lowudest us mide oðre monnes wouhwes."—*Ancren Riwle*, 190.

" Byuore Myhelmasse he was ycrouned þre *dawes* & nan mo."—*Rob. of Glouc.* 383.

"Suche mawmetys he hade yn hys *dawe*.—*Constitutions of Masonry*, p. 31, l. 509.

Done of Dawes = taken from day = killed,

" And alle *done of dawez* with dynttez of swreddez,"—*Morte Arthure* (ed. Perry), p. 61, l. 2056.

" ȝyf þou do any man o *dawe*."—*Rob. of Brunne Handlynge of Synne*, p. 34, l. 1034.

Is glossed " to the deþ."

The seventeenth century phrase, " done to death," is an echo of the older idiom.

l. 11. *Preste curatoure* = Priest who has cure of souls. These directions are only meant for such as have to take part in active ministrations; they relate to the priest's duties to a flock, not to the church, or his own soul.

P. 2, l. 23. The chastity here meant includes not only abstinence *ab illicitis*, but also from wedlock. When this treatise was written, the Church in England had long refused its sanction to the marriage of persons in holy orders. Though it was contrary to the theory of the Western Church from very early days, there is the most positive evidence that before the Norman Conquest English priests were frequently married. In the North of England celibacy was the exception rather than the rule. A clerical family, whose pedigree has been compiled by Mr. Raine (*Priory of Hexham*, Surtees Soc., v. i. p. li.) held the office of Priest of Hexham from father and son for several generations. Priests' children constantly occur in mediæval records, *e.g.* in William Painell's conformation charter to the nuns of Gokewell (The well of the Cuckoo) executed within a century of the Conquest, mention is made of " unum molendinum quod fuit Rodberti filii presbiteri" (*Linc. Arch. Soc. Rep.*, 1854, p. 102). The decrees of provincial councils show that priestly concubinage was in practice down to the period of the Reformation. The issue of such unions must have been sufficiently numerous to attract attention, for we find in 1281 the constitutions of Archbishop Peckham providing that priests' children should not succeed to their father's benefices, "absque dispensatione apostolica" (Wilkins, *Conc.* ii. 60). Strange things are told of dispensations, yet some will hardly believe Rycharde Layton, when he says of Jenyn, the last Prior of Maiden Bradley in Wiltshire, that, ".The pope, consideryng his fragilitie, gave him licens to kepe an hore, and [that he] hath goode writyng *sub plumbo* to discharge his conscience" (*Letters on Suppression of Monast.* Camd. Soc., p. 58). The tale is not incredible, but it comes from one whose words have slender authority. If the story be true, it speaks ill for the persons who were then ruling in matters spiritual, for Jenyn, after the suppression of his house, became rector of Shipton Moyne, Co. Gloucester.

l. 31. *Drokelec*, Dronkelewe. Drunkenness. A MS. of the 15th cent. (Add. 12195) bids folk take care that a nurse "be wysse and well a·ryssyd, and þat sche lof þe chylde, and þat sche be not *dronkeleche*."—*Prompt. Par.* i. 133. A piece of advice which is, I am informed, not entirely unneeded in these days. As to the termination *lac*, see Cockayne's *Seinte Marherete*, 101.

l. 43. *Pyked schone* came into use in the reign of William Rufus. It is said that the world owes this silly fashion to the ingenuity of Fulk, Earl of Anjou, who had deformed feet, and sought by this strange device to hide the defect from view. The pikes were sometimes made like the tails of scorpions, at others twisted into the form of a ram's horn. At a later period these long-toed boots were called cracowes from the belief that they were originally imported from Cracow. In Mr. C. R. Smith's collection of London Antiquities, now in the British Museum, are some shoes of this sort of the era of Edward IV.; the toes are six inches long and stuffed with moss. A long-toed patten was introduced for the use of persons who delighted in these fantastic habiliments. I presume this is alluded to in the *Detecta quædam in visitat. Eccl. Cath. Ebor.* A.D. 1390, where it is stated that "Omnes ministri Ecclesiæ pro majori parte, utuntur in Ecclesia et in processione *patens* et *clogges* contra honestatem Ecclesiæ et antiquam consuetudinem et ordinacionem capituli."—*Surtees' Soc.* 35, p. 243. The use of shoes of this sort was prohibited to the clergy by many local councils. See Du Frene, *Gloss. sub voc. Pigaciæ et Rostra*. Constitutions of London, A.D. 1342, in Wilkin's *Conc.* ii. 703. Fairholt's *Satirical Songs* on *Costume*, 43. Hewitt's *Ancient Armour*, i. 136.

l. 48. *Baselard*. A short sword worn by civilians in the fourteenth and fifteenth centuries. It is frequently shown on monumental effigies. A brass at King's Sombourne, Co. Hants., where one is represented, is engraved in Hewitt's *Ancient Armour and Weapons*, ii. 254. *Gent. Mag.* 1858, ii. 559. The Baselard was of two kinds—straight and curved. It was one of the former kind that Sir William Walworth presented to the Fishmongers' Company. The hooked or curved baselard was an eastern weapon (*Prompt. Par.* i. 25.) Capgrave tells us that Edmond Ironside was " slayn be the councel of Edrede, the duke; for he mad his son for to hide him undir a sege, where the King shuld voide, and sodeynly with a scharp *basulard* he smet the Kyng among the boweles."—*Chron.*, 125. By Statute 12, Richard II. c. vi. it was provided that, " null servant de husbandrie ou laborer ne servant de artificer ne de vitailler ne porte desore cnavant *baslard*, dagger, nespee sur forfaiture dicelle." Priests were strictly inhibited from wearing this instrument of war, but the rule was constantly broken.

"Bucklers brode, & swerdes long,
Baudrike, with *basclardes* kene,
Soch toles about her necke they hong:
With Antichrist soche priestes been."
—*Ploteman's Tale*, part 3.

That ordinances against the clergy wearing secular arms were not needless, is evident from many incidental notices in our records. On the 5th October, 1509, the Jury of the Manor of Kirton in Lindsey, presented that " Hugo Colynson capellanus vi & armis [*fecit*] affraiam super Will*ie*lmo ffreman & violent*er* extraxit sanguinem contra pacem do*m*ini regis." On the 22nd February, 1515, the same body, " dicunt quod Will*ie*lmus Brown Clericus pa*r*ochialis de Kyrtton vi & armis fec*it* affra*ia*m super Will*ie*lmo Wilkynson de Wadyngham" (*Rot. Cur.*). A satirical song of the early part of the 15th century, beginning—

" Prenegard, prenegard, thus bere I myn *basclard*,"

is printed in Fairholt's *Satirical Songs on Costume*, Percy Soc., p. 50.

l. 48. *Bawdryke.* Lat. *Baldrellus, Baldringus Baltheus.* French, *Baudrier.* A girdle or belt of any sort. It is used here for the swordbelt, probably for one of that kind that hangs over the right shoulder, and passes transversely across back and breast.

" Then þay schewed hym þe schelde, þat was of schyr goulez,
Wyth þe pentangel de-paynt of pure golde hewez;
He braydez hit by þe *baude-ryk*, a-boute þe hals kestes
þat bisemed þe segge semlyly fayre."
—*Sir Gawayne and the Green Knight*, p. 20, l. 621.

The *Baudrick* or *Baldryck* of a church bell was the whitleather thong, by which the clapper was suspended from the eye or staple in the crown of the bell. The word is of constant occurrence in old churchwardens' accounts.

[1428] Sol*uti* Thom*e* Basse pro j baudryk vj*d*.
—*Ch. Acc. St. Mary, Stamford*, Cotton MS. Vesp. A. 24, f, 3, b.
[1498] " Payd to John Clarke for makyng of a *bawdre* to ye bell, 1*d*."
[1502] " Payd to John Dalbe for *bavdree* makyng to þe belles, vi*d* "
—*Ch. Acc., Leverton, Co. Linc.*, MS. fol. 6, 8.
[15..] " Paid for makyng of a belle *batrey* and mending, viij*d*."
[1535] " Payd to roger codder for iij *bautres* making vi*d*."
—*Ch. Acc, Kirton in Lindsey*, MS. p. 14, 19.

l. 49. For illustrations of the history of the clerical tonsure consult Bingham, *Antiq. Christ. Church*, b. vj. c. iv. Rock, *Ch. of our Fathers*, v. i. p. 185. Lyndwood, *Provinciale*, lib. i. tit. 14, p. 69. Beda, *Eccl. Hist.* lib. v., c. xxi. Beyerlinck, *Magnum Theatrum Vitæ Humanæ* sub voc *Tonsura*. Martene, *De Antiq. Eccl. Rit.* (Venetiis, 1783), vol. ii. p. 14; vol. iii. p. 284, 293, 300, 335; vol. iv. p. 113, 174, 238, 274.

P. 3, l. 59. *Schrewes*. In the older English this word stands for enemies, wretches, or evil disposed persons of either sex.

> "Þe Cristene men leyde euere on, & slowe euere to grounde,
> Al clene þe *ssrewen* were ouercome in a stounde."

> "He adde endyng, as he wurþe was, & such yt ys to be a *ssrewe*."
> —*Rob. Glouc.* 407, 419.

> "Such qualité nath noman to bee lechour other *schrewe*."
> —*Pop. Treatises on Science*, p 133.

l. 82. *Hosele*, to administer the holy communion, A.S. *Husl*, an offering, an oblation, and hence the host, as the highest of all offerings. To housel was the ordinary name for the act of giving the communion until the period of the Reformation. From the earliest times, as far as we know, in this country the altar breads were in the form of wafers—thin and round cakes stamped with some sacred divice or monogram. That they differed from the coarse household bread of the people is indicated by the fact that the sons of Sabert (Sœberht) the Christian king of the East Saxons, *circa* 604, who had remained out of the Christian fold, when they asked Bishop Melitus, after their father's death, why he would not give them the eucharist of which he had been accustomed to partake, said, as we have their words reported to us in Latin, "quare non et nobis porrigis panem nitidum, quem et patri nostro dabas." Beda, *Hist. Eccl.* lib. ii. c. 5. These altar breads were frequently called *obleys*. Lat. *oblata*. It is believed that they were usually made by nuns, or anchoresses. It was so certainly in the ninth century in France. There is a tale told in a contemporary life of St. Wandragesilius, Abbot of Fontenelle, a Benedictine monastery on the Seine, near Rouen, of a certain nun who went to the fire for the purpose of baking this bread, holding in her hand the iron stamps for the purpose. "Accessit ad ignem, ferroque quo imprimendæ ac decoquendæ erant oblatæ, arrepto, mox nervi manus ejus dexteræ contracti sunt, ac oblatorium quod sponte susceperat, invita, vi agente divina retinuit." *Acta Sanct.* Julii t. v. p. 290 n. 53. As quoted in Rock. *Ch. of our Fathers*, v. i. p. 152.

The altar breads were of two kinds. The larger, called singing-bread, were used for the sacrifice; the smaller, called houseling-bread, were used for the communion of the people. They were sometimes kept for sale by country shopkeepers (*Gent. Mag.*, 1864, pt. ii.

p. 502). There is preserved in the Rotuli Parliamentorum, 1472-3, a curious petition from Johanna Glyn, widow of John Glyn, of Morvale, in the county of Cornwall, gentleman, in which she complains of the bad treatment her late husband had received from the hands of certain rioters. Among other things she says, "The said Riottours, the same day and place toke the said John Glyn and hym ymprisoned, and in the Castell, in prisone hym kept by the space of v oures, and more, so that noon of his frendes myght come where he was to releve hym with drynk, or staunche his bloode, to th'entent that he shuld have bled to deth, except they suffered a Preste to come to shryve and *howsell* hym."—Vol. vj. p. 35.

In the *Privy Purse expences of Henry viij.* are several entries similar to the following, the interpretation of which has been held to present a difficulty:—"I*te*m the x daye [of April, 1530] paied to maist*er* Weston by way of the king*es* rewarde ayenst easter, xx*s*." "I*te*m the same daye, paied by lyke rewarde to the two guilliams and phillippes boye for ther *howsell*, x*s*. a pece, xxx*s*." p. 38 *cf.* 40, 41, 330. There can be no doubt that the meaning is, that the king presented to the persons named x*s*. for them to give as an offering at their Easter communion.

The little bell, which it was the practice to ring before the holy eucharist when the priest took it to the sick, was called a *howslinge* bell. See Peacock's *Eng. Church Furniture*, p. 86. Housel-sippings was the unconsecrated wine which was given at certain times to the lay folk out of the chalice. Bishop John Bale says, "They will pay no more money for the *housel*-sippings, bottom blessings, nor for seyst me and seyst me not above the head and under of their chalices. —*Image of both Churches*, edit. 1849, p. 526.

A *houseling-towel* or *houseling-cloth*, was the linen sheet used when the holy communion was received for the purpose of hindering particles thereof from falling on the ground. "A *howslyng* tewell, off dyaper, w*ith* blew melyngs atte the ende, goode."—*Ch. Goods, St. Dunstan's Canterbury. Gent. Mag.*, 1837, pt. 2, p. 570. A cloth of this kind was employed at royal coronations until recent times. That of William IV. was the first where it was disused.—Maskell, *Mon. Rit.* iii. 834.

l. 87. Midwives were licenced by the bishop of the diocese. These licences continued to be issued till long after the Reformation. The form may be seen in Strype's *Annals*, vol. i. p. 242. In Grindal's *Articles to be enquired into in the Province of Canterbury*, A.D. 1576, the fifty-eighth question is, "Whether there be any among you that use sorcery, or witchcraft, or that be suspected of the same, and whether any use any charmes or unlawful prayers, or invocations in Latin or otherwise, and, namely, midwives in the time of woman's travail of child, and whether any do resort to any such help or counsel, and what be their names."—Grindal's *Remains*, p. 174.

In Bale's *Comedye concerninge thre Lawes*, 1528, sig. B. iii. b.

as quoted in Brande's *Pop. Antiq.*, 1813, v. ii. p. 5, we have a notice of some of the superstitious doings of midwives.

> " Yea, but now ych am a she,
> And a good mydwyfe perde,
> Yonge chyldren can I charme,
> With whysperynges and whysshynges,
> With crossynges and with kyssynges,
> With blasynges and with blessynges,
> That spretes do them no harm."

Midwives sometimes murdered children for purposes of magic. Sprenger in his *Malleus Malificarum*, v. 2, as quoted in Beyerlinck, *Mag. Theat. Vitæ Humanæ*, v. vij. p. 784, b. tells us of the burning of two women of this class, "quia earum vna quadraginta altera innumerabiles pueros recens in lucem editos necavissent, inditis clam in eorum capita grandibus aciculis."

P. 4, l. 95. De baptismo infantium, quos mater in partu laborans, in lucem emittere non valet, ita definiunt antiqua Statuta Synodalia Ecclesiæ Nemausiensis [Nismes] .... Si vero, muliere in partu laborante, infans extra ventrem matris caput tantum emiserit, et in tanto periculo infans posjtus nasci nequiverit, infundant aliqua de obstetricibus aquam super caput infantis dicens, 'Ego baptizo te in nomine Patris,' etc., et erit baptizatus. His concinunt Statuta Synodalia ecclesiæ Biterrensis a Guillelmo episcopo anno 1342 edita .... ab hac sententia non nihil deflectunt Statuta antiqua ecclesiæ Ruthensis. Sic enim habent capite sexto: Si vero, muliere in partu laborante infans extra ventrem matris caput tantum emiserit, et in tanto periculo infans positus commode haberi nequiverit, infundet aliquis vel aqua de astantibus aquam super caput infantis dicens. 'Creatura Dei, ego te baptizo in nomine Patris, & Filii, & Spiritus sancti.' Et erit baptizatus."—Martene, *De Antiq. Eccl. Rit.* i. 58, 59, where much more relating to this subject may be seen.

In the consistorial acts of the Diocese of Rochester, the following document relative to the baptism of a child during birth is preserved. I quote from the *Gentleman's Mag.* 1785, pt. ii, p. 939.

"1523, Oct. 14. *Elizabeth* Gaynsford obstetrix examinata dicit in vim juramenti sui sub hâc formâ verborum. I, the aforesaid Elizabeth, seeing the childe of Thomas Everey, late born in jeapardy of life, by the authorite of my office, then beyng midwife, dyd christen the same childe under this manner, In the name of the Fader, the Son, and the Holy Ghost, I christen thee, Denys, iffundend*am* meram aquam super caput infantuli. Intorrogata erat, Whether the childe was born and delivered from the wyfe of the said Thomas? Whereto she answereth and saith, that the childe was not born, for she saw nothyng of the childe but the hedde, and for the perell the childe was in, and in that tyme of nede, she christened as is aforesaid, and cast water with her hand on the childes hede. After which so done, the childe was born, and was had to the churche, where the Priest gave to it that chrystynden that lakkyd, and the childe is yet alyf."

l. 116. In cases of necessity it was permitted to baptize in a wooden vessel, which was to be burned when the ceremony was over, to prevent its being used for secular purposes hereafter. Martene, *De Antiq. Eccl. Rit.* i. 5.

l. 120. *Nuye,* Annoy, trouble. Old Fr. *Anoi* from Lat. *Odium.*

" And a ryche man hyt *noyeþ* oftyn tyde
Þat a pore man hat oghte besyde."
—*Rob. of Brunne, Handlynge Synne,* p. 187, l. 5981.

P. 5, l. 133. *On rowe,* in order. A.S. *Rawa.*

" He rehersed be *rowe* the rite of Edgare."
—Capgrave, *Chron.* 172.

The gild of St. Mary of Boston had, in 1534, a corporal, which was in part made of *rawed* satten of brigges," *i.e.* satin made in rows or stripes. The editor's *Church Furniture,* p. 205. Lincolnshire people still speak of Turnip *raws.*

l. 143. Fonts were usually only blessed at Easter and Whitsuntide. When the service of blessing was performed, they were vested in a linen cloth. Martene, *De Antiq. Eccl. Rit.* iii. 150. Maskell, *Mon. Rit.* i. 13, where the service may be found.

l. 153. See exhortation in the Salisbury *Ordo ad faciendum Catechumenum.* Maskell, *Mon. Rit.* i. 14. On the font at Bradley, Co. Lincoln, is inscribed, "Pater noster abe maria and crede leren ye chyld yt es nede." The inscription is coeval with the font, *i.e.* circa A.D. 1500.

l. 155. "Inhibemus sub poena excommunicationis, ne aliquae mulieres vel uxores parvulos suos in lectulis suis secum collocari permittant, antequam ætatis suæ tertium annum impleverint. Quod statutum ad minus semel in anno singulis sacerdotibus volumus promulgari."—*Constitutiones synodales Sodorenses,* A.D. 1291. Cap xiv. in Wilkins' *Conc.* ii. 177.

P. 7, l. 203. "Debet enim sacerdos *banna* in facie ecclesiæ infra missarum solemnia cum major populi adfuerit multitudo, per tres dies solemnes et disjunctas interrogare: ita ut inter unumquemque diem solemnem cadat ad minus una dies ferialis. Rubric in *Ordo ad faciendum Sponsalia.*" Maskell, *Mon. Rit.* i. 44. In Lincolnshire the *banns* of marriage are called spurrings, *i.e.* askings, from *Spere,* to enquire; A.S. *Spyrian,* to track; Dutch, *Speuren*; Germ. *Spuren.*

In the ancient office the earlier part of the rite took place, "ante ostium ecclesiæ coram Deo sacerdote et populo."

" Husbonds at chirche dore have I had fiue,
For I so often haue I-wedded be."
—Chaucer, *Wife of Bath, Prolog.*

Martene has published from an ancient manual of the diocese of

Rheims the following verses, to aid in calling to mind the different hindrances to wedlock:

> " Error, conditio, votum, cognatio, crimen,
> Cultus desparitas, ordo, ligamen, honestas,
> Si sis affinis, sique coiere nequis."
> —*De Antiq. Eccl. Rit.* ii. 137.

P. 8, l. 241. It was in the Middle Ages, as at present, a matter of obligation for all Catholics to receive the holy communion at Easter-tide.

l. 247. *Ded*, death, a common provincialism. A Lincolnshire woman told the editor that she "would rather be nibbled to *dead* with ducks, than live with Miss ——; she is always a nattering."

l. 252. After communion it was the custom for the laity to drink unconsecrated wine, to assist them in swallowing the eucharistic wafer. The purchase of wine for this use sometimes appears in old accounts, and has led to the mistaken notion that it was a common practice in those days to give the communion in both kinds. The following passage from the account rolls of Coldingham is peculiarly liable to this misconstruction. 1364. "In vino empto per annum pro celebracione et pro communione parochianorum ad Pascham xv$^{s.}$ i$^{d.}$" p. xliv, as quoted in Rock's *Ch. of our Fathers*, iii. pt. 2, p. 170. In the constitutions of Archbishop Peckham, promulgated in 1281, this practice is described in words, of which the text is a simple translation. "Doceant [sacerdotes] etiam eosdem illud, quod ipsis eisdem temporibus in calice propinatur, sacramentum non esse, sed vinum purum eis hauriendum, traditum, ut facilius sacrum corpus glutiant quod perceperunt." Wilkins, *Conc.* ii. 52. It was ordained by the Synod of Exeter, A.D. 1287, that there should be in every church as well as the chalice employed in saying mass, a cup of silver or tin to be used when communion was given to the sick. In this cup the priest washed his fingers, and the sick man, after he had communicated, drunk the water. *Ibid.* ii. 139. The "device for the coronation of King Henry vij." published among the Rutland Papers (Camd. Soc.) p. 22, shows that he and his queen partook of a chalice of this kind at that high ceremony.

P. 9, l. 260. *Sad*, gravely. "He [Maurice, Lord Berkeley, born 1457] was called by writ to the state of a Baron, and recommended to provide a *sadd* gentlewoman in Court to wait upon my lady."—Forbroke's *Smith's Lives of the Berkeleys*, 175.

> "But ye .... vse .... to loke so *sadly* whan ye mene merely yt many times men dowbte whyther ye speke in Sporte whan ye mene good ernest."—*Sir Th. More, Workes*, 1557, p. 127 b.

l. 267. *Bordes*, Jests, games; Fr. *Bourde*; Dutch, *Boerde*; Lat. *Burdare*, to jest.

> " And y shal telle as y kan,
> A *bourde* of an holy man."
> —*R. of Brunne, Handlyng of Synne*, p. 287, l. 9260.

"We have so mocked him with his gospel that we shall find it is no *bourding* with him."—*John Bradford's Works*, v. i. p. 38.

"*Bourd* not wi' bawtie."—Scottish proverb, Ramsay's *Reminiscences of Scottish Life*, ii edit. 139.

"The sooth *bourd* is nae *bourd*."

—Scottish proverb, *Redgauntlet*, ch. xi.

l. 270. We have evidence here that at the time this poem was written, it was not a common thing for people to sit on benches in church. Nearly all the pre-reformation church seats in existence in this country are of the late perpendicular era. Pews were, however, in common use before the Reformation. Sir Thomas More frequently makes mention of them in such a manner as to shew that they were no novelties to him. He tells us "how men fell at varyance for kissing of the pax, or goyng before in procession, or setting of their wiues pewes in the church." We may surmise from this that pews were sometimes restricted to women. A pew seems, from the following story, to have been the eminence upon which offenders did public penance. "These witnes in dede will not lye; As the pore man sayd by the priest, if I may be homely to tell you a mery tale by the way. A mery tale, quod I, commith neuer amyse to me. The pore man quod he had founde ye priest ouer famyliar with his wife, and bycause he spake of it a brode and coulde not proue it, the priest sued him before ye bishoppes offyciall for dyffamatyon where the pore man vpon paine of cursynge was commaunded that in his paryshe chyrche, he should upon ye sondaye, at high masse time stande vp & sai, 'mouth, thou lyest.' Wherupon for fulfilling of hys penance, vp was the pore soule set in a pew, that ye peple might wonder on him and hyre what he sayd. And there all a lowed, (whan he had rehersyd what he had reportyd by the priest) than he sett hes handys on his mouth and said, 'mouth! mouth, thou lyest.' And by and by therupon he set his hand vpon both his eyen & sayd, 'but eyen, eyen,' quod he, 'by ye mass ye lie not a whitte.'" pp. 88, *c*. 127, *d*.

l. 272. In Durham *sitting on the knees* is an expression still used for kneeling.

l. 273.   *Flat* = Floor.

"A hep of girles sittende aboute the *flet*."

—Wright's *Political Songs*, Camd. Soc. p. 337.

The floors of the houses in Edinburgh, where each floor is the home of a separate family, are called *flats*. Houses containing only one family as occupants are known as "houses within themselves." See Scott's *Guy Mannering*, xxxvi. The warp on each side of the River Trent, that is, submerged by the tide, is called The Trent *Flat*. On the Lincolnshire coast, the low land on the shore is often named the *Flat*, as Sand Hall *Flat*, near Tetney Haven, and Friskney *Flat*.

l. 280. *Blesse.* That is, make the sign of the cross. This act is still called blessing one's-self by Catholics.

"The Apostles and Fathers of the Primitive Church blessed themselves with the sign of the cross." John Marshall, as quoted by Fulke. Fulke's Works (Parker Soc.) ii. 171.

"Blest themselves with both hands" is Sir Thomas Urquhart's version of "se signoient, de toutes mains." Rabelais, *Gargantua*, b. 1, c. xxxv.

l. 281. The versicle said immediately before the Gospel, in the Ancient English as in the Roman Mass, is, *Gloria tibi, Domine*.

l. 284. The sanctus sance or sauce bell was a small bell usually hung outside the church in a little hutch or cote on the east gable of the nave. This was rung at the elevation of the host in the parish mass, to warn all those who were not present at the service to join their hearts with the devotions of the worshippers. The sacring bell was a smaller bell of this kind, to be rung at other masses. It was sometimes hung in the rood loft; more commonly it was, as it is at present in Roman Catholic churches, merely a handbell. Handbells and sacring bells were among the things ordered to "be utterly defaced, rent, and abolished," in 1576. Grendal's *Remains*, p. 159. They were mostly destroyed in Lincolnshire in or before A.D. 1566. See editor's *Church Furniture*, passim.

P. 10, l. 309. "Cum autem ad infirmum eucharistia deportatur, ita decenter se habeant portatores, superpelliciis saltem induti, cum campanella, lumine præcedente, nisi vel aëris intemperies obstet vel loci remotio; ut per hoc devotio fidelium augeatur, qui Salvatorem suum tenentur in via, luto non obstante, flexis genibus adorare, ad quod sunt per sacerdotes suos attentius commonendi. W. de Cantilupe, *Constit.* A.D. 1240. In Wilkins' *Conc.* i. 667.

l. 315. After long search I have failed to find any passage similar to this in the writings of Augustinus. I am informed by two persons, who have made the writings of this saint an object of especial study, that no such statements occur in them.

P. 11, l. 328. *Seyntuary*, churchyard. The name of sanctuary is now given to that part of the choir or chancel of a church where the altar stands. In mediæval documents belonging to this country, *Sanctuarium* and its equivalents in English almost always mean churchyard. "Ecclesiarum *Sanctuaria*, quæ populariter coemeteria nominantur." *Stat. Cicest.* in Wilkins' *Conc.* ii. 183. *Chirch hay*, churchyard. A.S. *Cyrce*, church, *Heg*, hay, grass, or *Hege*, a hedge, or fence.

l. 332. Games and secular business were forbidden in churchyards by the Synod of Exeter, A.D. 1287. Wilkins, *Conc.* ii. 140. By 12 Ric. II. c. vi. servants were ordered to amuse themselves with bows and arrows on Sundays, and to give up foot-ball, quoits, casting the stone, "keyles," and other such inopportune games. In consequence of this statute the jury of the manor of Kirton in Lindsey, 4th April, 1 Henry viij. made a presentment that "Will*iel*mus Welton " se male gessit in ludendo ad pilam pedalem et alia joca illicita."—*Rot. Cur.*

l. 332, *n. Stoil ball*, stool-ball. This game is still played in

Sussex. There is a description of it in *Notes and Queries*, iii. s. xi. 457.

l. 338. The holding of fairs and markets in churchyards was made illegal by statute in 1285. *Stat. Winhest.* 13 *Edw.* I. c. vj. The practice, however, of using churches and churchyards for secular purposes continued to be common. Edward I. received the oaths of the competitors for the Crown of Scotland in Norham Church. In 1326 the tythe corn of Fenham, Fenwick, and Beele was collected in the chapel at Fenham, and at about the same period, when the monks of Holy Island found their grange would hold no more, they converted the chapel attached to their manse into a temporary tythe barn. Raine's *North Durham*, 82, 260. Law Courts were held, books sold, and children taught in the porch of St. Peter's, Sandwich. Boys' *Hist. Sandw.* 365. A manor court, called Temple court, was held in the church of St. Mary, and St. John Baptist, Dunwich, annually on the feast of All Souls.—Gardner's *Dunwich*, 54. Wool was stored in one of the churches at Southampton. J. T. Rogers, *Hist. of Agriculture*, i. 32; ii. 611; and a law-suit settled in St. Peter's Church, Bristol. Fosbroke's *Smith's Lives of the Berkeleys*, 92. In 1519 Pedlars were accustomed, on feast days, to sell their wares in the church porch of Ricall, Co. York.—*Surtees Soc.* 35, p. 271.

l. 338. *Chost*. A.S. *Ceást*, strife.

"& mad tille him feaute, withouten any *chest*,
& cleymed him for þer chefe of West & of Est."
—*Langtoft Chron.* 19.

l. 353. Old Norse, *Naut*, an ox. A.S. *Nyten*, an animal, from *nitan* (*ne witan*), not to know. Scotch, *Nolt*.

P. 12, l. 358. *Fonne*, a fool. *Fond* = foolish is a Lincolnshire provincialism.

l. 360. *Telyng* means, as I conceive, rhythmical couplets or verses intended to charm away evil or cause good luck.

l. 366. *Gart*, third pers. sing. of *Gare*, to cause. O.N. *göra, gera*. A.S. *Gearwian*. Mod. Scotch, *Gar*.

"My precios perle dotȝ me gret pyne,
What serueȝ tresor, bot gareȝ men grete."
—*Allit. Poems*, E.E.T.S. p. 11, l. 330.

The following inscription wrought in stained glass once decorated a window in the church of Blyton, Co. Linc.:

"Prieȝ for ye gilð of Corpus Ypi quilk ᵱis window garte mak."
—*Harl. MS.* 6829, f. 198.

A mediæval bell still hangs in the church tower of Alkborough, a little Lincolnshire village near the point where the Trent falls into the Humber, on which is inscribed + Jesu : for : yt : modir : sake : sabe : al : the : sauls : that : me : gart : make : amen.

l. 368. The following charm is worth reprinting here as it occurs in a book where no one would think of looking for it. Hooper, the

Reformer, says that he knew a poor man who had it in his possession, vainly hoping that it could heal all diseases.

+ Jesus + Job + habuit + vermes + Job + patitur + vermes + in + nomine + Patris + et + Filii + et + Spiritus Sancti + amen + lama + zabacthani + —*Early Writings*, Parker Soc. 328.

l. 372. *Okere*, usury. A S. *Eácan*, to augment. Old Norse, *Okr*. Goth. *Aukan*. Usury has been a subject for much angry and protracted discussion. See Lecky's *Hist. Rationalism*, j. *passim*. The *Catechism of the Council of Trent* says, "Whatever is received above the principal, be it money, or anything else that may be purchased by money is usury." Pt. iij. chap. viij. quest xj· Donovan's *Translat*. Grindal's *Injunctions* of 1571, class usurers with "adulterers, fornicators, incestuous persons," and other like notorious criminals. They define usurers to be "all those who lend money, corn, ware, or other thing, and receive gain therefore over and above that which is lent." *Remains*, 143. The imaginative literature of former times contains many stories of the unhappy fate of usurers. See for a copious collection of them, Beyerlinck, *Mag. Theat. Vitæ Humanæ*. v. vij. p. 1064.

In 1644 the churchwardens of Kirton in Lindsey put out money at eight per cent.; they note among their receipts, "William Kent, gent*le*man, for 5 li vpon a bond 8s."—*Church Accounts, MS*. 197.

P. 13, l. 394. *Blyue*, quickly.

"Heo hadde þe maistry of þe feld, þe Romaynes flow *blyue*."
—*Rob. Glouc*. p. 50 n.

"The kyng issued fro his navee *bliue*."
—*Romans of Partenay*, p. 195, l. 5673.

l. 411. *Steuene*, voice. A.S. *Stefen*.

"Whan Litle John heard his master speake,
Well knew he it was his *steven*."
—*Robin Hood and Guy of Gisb*. l. 210.

l. 419. *Gult*, trespass, guilt.

"Forȝif us our *gultes*, also we forȝifet oure gultare,"
—Maskell, *Mon. Rit*. ij. 238.

l. 420. *Fondynge*. A.S. *Fandian*, to try.

"Leod us in tol na *fandinge*."
—MS. *Cot. Cleop*. B. vj. f. 201 in Maskell, *Mon. Rit*. ij. 238.

"Lat us nouȝt be *fonded* in sinne."
—MS. *Bibl. Reg*. 5 c. v. as above, ij. 239.

l. 422. The "Hail Mary," as at present used by Roman Catholics, was unknown in mediæval England. I believe the Sarum Breviary of 1531 is the earliest authority for the modern form. The Salisbury Primer of 1556 breaks off at the same point as the prayer in the text. Dr. Rock gives a most interesting dissertation on this prayer in his *Church of our Fathers*, iii. pt. i. p. 315.

P. 16, l. 499. *Dele*, Part. A.S. *Dǽl*, Part. Sanse. *Dal*, to split;

hence, *Deal* and *Dole*, to distribute. *Deal*, a plank or separated piece of wood. *Deal*, at cards. *Dole*, money, food, or raiment given by way of alms; to *Deal* in the way of traffic or merchandize, and, as I think, *Dale* and *Dell*, a valley. Before the enclosures in Lincolnshire the word *Dale* was frequently used to describe the shares of land which the freeholders and copyholders had in the open fields; this word was constantly employed when the portions of land were in such positions that they could not in any way be considered as valleys, *e.g.* Dimmore dale, Bachester dale, Northorpe gate dale, Black moulde dale, Baytinge cross dale, Dale extra bori*alem* de slump cross, Beacon dale, Mount dale, and 2 dales iux*ta* molendin*um*, in the parish of Kirton in Lindsey. Norden and Thorpe's Survey of Kirton Soke, *MS. Pub. Lib. Cantab.* Ff. 4, 30. fol. 7.

"So þat þe meste *del* of hey men þat in Englond beþ
Beþ ycome of þe Normans."
—*Rob. Glouc.* 368.

"His mayster loved hym so welle,
He fette hym gold every *delle.*"
—*Child of Bristow, Retrosp. Rev.* Feb. 1854, p. 204.

"*Deal* on, *deal* on, my merry men, all,
Deal on your cake and your wine,
For whatever is *dealt* at her funeral day,
Shall be dealt to-morrow at mine."
—*Marg. and Will. Percy Relics.*

"He turn'd his face unto the wa'
And death was with him *dealan*,
Adiew! adiew! my dear friends a'
Be kind to Barbara Allan."
—*Sir John Grehene and Barbara Allan, Percy's Relics.*

P. 18, l. 582. The holy oils used in the Catholic Church were of three kinds—*oleum sanctum, oleum chrismatis, et oleum informorum.* With the *oleum sanctum*, the creme of the text, the child was anointed on the breast and between the shoulders, during the introductory part of the baptismal service ere it was plunged in the font or sprinkled with water. When the baptism proper was over it was anointed on the head in the form of a cross with *oleum. chrismatis* or creme. The *oleum informorum*, or sick men's oil, was the oil used in the service of extreme unction. The oil used for this purpose was made from olives. With the chrism was mingled sweet-smelling balsam. The consecration took place on Holy Thursday. Maskell, *Mon. Rit.* i. 22. Rock, *Ch. of our Fathers*, iij. pt. ij. p. 79. The three little bottles in which these oils were preserved were kept in a box called a chrismatory. This little chest was usually oblong in form, with a crested lid, somewhat like the Noah's Arks children are wont to play with. It was often called an oynting-box, oil-box, or creme-box.

l. 585. *Ore*, grace, mercy. Old Norse, *eira*.
"Cryde hym mylce & *ore*."
—*Rob. Glouc.* 381.

P. 20. l. 651. }*erne*, earnestly. A.S. *Georne*.
"He bed him }*erne* vor to a bide."
—*Rob. Glouc.* 487.

l. 654. The sacrament of confirmation can, in ordinary cases, be administered by a bishop only. In some instances this power has been delegated to a priest. At these times the oil has been blessed by one of the episcopal order.

l. 660. *Stoke.* A.S. *Stoc*, a stake, from *stingan*, to thrust in, to prick, to sting. Dut. and Ger. *Stock*. Fr. *Estoc*. Ital. *Stocco*. Lat. *Truncus*. Hence, *Holy-Water-Stock*, the pillar or post on which the holy water vessel was fixed. The *Stocks*, an instrument of correction. *Stocks*, the frame on which a ship is built. *Stocks*, public monies. *Stock*, a race or family. *Stock*, the store or fixed things on a farm. *Stock*, the stiff bandage round the neck. To *stock*, a North country word for to bar or bolt a door. *Stock-Lock*, a lock fixed upon a door. *Stock*, the handle of any thing. *Stook*, twelve sheaves of corn *stuck* upright, their upper ends inclining towards each other like a high pitched roof. *Stock-Dove*, the dove that lives in trees. *Stoothes*, thin spars of wood used in house building. *Stoccade*, a fence of stakes. *Stock*, a gilliflower, so called, says Skinner, "quia tum radix tum caulis instar ligni solida et dura sunt." *Stoker*, a man who sticks, *i.e.* pushes, pokes, or stirs the fire. *Stockfish*, so called "quia durus est instar *Stocci*, *i.e.* Trunci seu Caudicis," or because it is so hard that it requires beating with a stick to make it fit for eating. *Stocken*, a Lincolnshire word, signifying stopped in growth, choked with food or filled with water, as a sponge; and the family names of *Stock*, *Stocks*, and *Stookes*.

"A hallie water *stocke* of stone at the church dore with a sprinckle of a stick."— 1566. *Ch. Goods Destroyed at Gretford*. Peacock's *Ch. Furniture*, 91.

[1579]. "Payd to James battman xijs. ixd., by the collectors, for the poore, wich was layd owt of the common *stook* befor for Gouldes childe."—*Kirton in Lindsey Ch. Accts.* p. 71.

[1419]. "In xxiiij. paribus ligaturarum ferri cum uncis et V *stokloks* ab eodem emptis, 10s. 4d."—*Fabric Rolls of York Minster*, 38.

[1519.] "Oftyn tymes the dure is *stokked*, and we parsons & vicars cannot get brede, wyne, nor water."—*Ibid.* 268.

[1641]. "Those that binde and *stooke* are likewise to have 8d. a day, for bindinge and *stookinge* of winter corne is a man's labour."—Best's *Farming Book*, 43.

[1552-3]. "For settinge in ij. *stothes* and mendyng the wall of the receiver's chalmer over the stare."—Howden Roll, 5-6 Edward VI. Quoted in *Fabric Rolls of York Minster*, 355.

P. 21, l. 663. The person confirmed was anointed with chrism, in the form of a cross; afterwards, out of reverence for the chrism, the forehead was bandaged with a white linen band. The *Ordo Romanus* provides that this ligature should be worn for seven days. This was supposed to shadow forth the seven-fold gifts of the Holy Ghost, conferred by the rite; " Spiritus sapientiæ et intellectus, Spiritus consilii et fortitudinis, Spiritus scientiæ et pietatis et Spiritus timoris Domini." The length of time these fillets were retained varied in different places. The Council of Worcester, A.D. 1240, provided that they should be worn but three days. This is stated to have been in honour of the Trinity. They were to be removed in church by the priest, who was instructed to wash the foreheads of the confirmed, and to pour the water into the font. The bandages were usually ordered to be burnt. In some cases, however, it seems that they were reserved to be used as napkins for the priest to wipe his hands upon after using the holy oils. " Vero ad humanos usus nullatenus transferatur, sed comburatur, vel in usus muridos ecclesiæ deputetur." This passage is glossed, "Forte ad abstergendas manus post sacrorum oleorum contrectationem."—Martene, *De Antiq. Eccl. Rit.* i. 92; iv. 417.

l. 684. The English form of the greater excommunication, reprinted by Mr. Maskell, *Mon. Rit.* ij. 286, differs in many particulars from the one here given. It is much longer. I have not succeeded in discovering any Latin form that tallies in all particulars with the one in the text. It is probable that each diocese possessed its own special cursing service, and that this varied from time to time in accordance with the fluctuations of the sins of the people. Several Latin forms of this nature have been printed by Wilkins, *Conc.* ij. 29, 35, 56, 161, 240, 300, 678, and Martene, *De Antiq. Eccl. Rit.* ij. 314, 322, 325.

P. 22, l. 711. The use of fraudulent measures and weights was most severely punished in the Middle Ages. There was perhaps not a country in Europe where the rogues who resorted to these practices were exempt from excommunication. Certainly there was no part of the civilized world where the State dealt so leniently with this form of oppression of the poor as it does in Britain at present. In these matters we were far wiser four hundred years ago. Here is a specimen of a manner in which the Londoners of old time handled criminals of this class :—

"If any default shall be found in the bread of a baker of the city, the first time, let him be drawn upon a hurdle from the Guildhall to his own house, through the great streets where there may be most people assembled, and through the great streets that are most dirty, with the faulty loaf hanging from his neck. If a second time he shall be found committing the same offence, let him be drawn through the great street of Chepe, in manner aforesaid, to the pillory; and let him be put upon the pillory, and remain there at least one hour in the day. And the third [time that such] default shall be found, he shall be drawn, and the oven shall be pulled down, and the baker [made to] foreswear the trade within the city for ever." *Liber Albus*, book iij. pt. ij. p. 265. I have used Mr. Riley's translation, p. 232.

All measures in London were to be sealed by the alderman of the ward in which the user dwelt, either with his own private seal or the seal of the chamber. If any measures were found upon trial to be smaller than they should be, they were to be burnt forthwith in the chief street of the ward, and the name of the culprit who had used them was to be presented to the chamberlain that he might be fined.—*Ibid.* 290.

Manor courts have exercised the right of assize of bread and ale from very ancient times. The practise has not yet been abolished by statute. The charge to the Court Leet Jury, as given by William Sheppard, in his *Court Keeper's Guide*, 2nd edit., 1650, contains the following passages:—" You are to inquire of deceits and other offences in trade and traffique, and such as are imployed therein; of all such as either make or sell deceitfull wares, or use deceit in that they sell; as if a butcher blow up his meat, or the like; or if a tradesman sell by false weights and measures, or by two; that buy by greater and sell by lesser measures; or if bakers and brewers keep not the assize, the prices, and quantities, according to the writing of the Marshalsie, that either sel lesse in weight or measure, or take more in price then is set down. For these offences they are to be amerced as you shall think fit. . . . . . If any baker in any city, town, corporate, or market town, make or sell any horse-bread which is not of lawfull assize, and a reasonable weight, after the price of corn and grain in the market adjoining; or if any hostler, or Inholder, dwelling in any city, &c., make horse-bread in his hostrie, or without, or not sell their horse-bread, and their hay, oats, beans, pease, provender, and all kinde of victuall, both for man and beast, for reasonable gain." 51-53. On the ale-taster of each manor devolved the duty of regulating the assize of bread and ale. The oath which he took may be seen in Sir William Scoggs' *Practise of Court-Leet*, 1714, p. 15.

The following is a specimen of the manner in which the fines for breaches of the bread and ale assize were usually entered in court rolls. The editor quotes from the records of the manor of Bottesford, Co. Lincoln, of which he is the lord. He is sorry to add that the good practice here recorded has long fallen into disuse, though the evil it was intended to remedy still exists.

[1569]. "De v*x*ore Rober*ti* Symond quia ven*didit* scre*viciam* & pane*m* con*tra* ass*isam*, ij*s*."

There are few things more wanted by antiquaries than a good treatise on the weights and measures of the Middle Ages. They differed almost in every county, often in adjoining parishes. In the Isle of Axholme, and other parts of the Hundreds of Manley and Corringham, a bushel is not, as elsewhere, one-eighth of a quarter, but double that measure. The *strike* or half-bushel represents there the legal bushel of eight pecks. The following is the earliest instance of the use of this local measure I have seen. Its origin is, no doubt, much more remote. In the time of Edward VI., the precise year not noted, the churchwardens of Kirton in Lindsey sold sundry parcels of "lyane," line, or flax seed.

> " To thomas Smyth, of brege, iii. q*uartores*, iiij*s*.
> to willia*m* redar, of ye same, i. q*uar*tor, xvj*d*.
> to R*y*c*hard* Hamsto*n*, a bowyssyll, iiij*d*.
> to þe glover of ba*r*to*n*, a bowyssyll, iiij*d*.
>   .   .   .   .   .   .
> to R*y*c*hard* Parkyng, of Asbey, ij. q*uar*tor*es* haly*f*, iij*s*. iiij*d*.
> to þe glower of hebarstowe, half a q*uar*ter, viij*d*."
> —*Kirton in Lindsey Ch. Accts.* p. 13.

l. 716. This was no doubt levelled against all persons bearing false witness against wills; but was especially directed against those who made false statements regarding nuncupative wills. These verbal testaments were very common in the Middle Ages. They had to be proved in the spiritual court of the diocese by persons who had been present at their making, and were from the absence of written record; and the fact that the testator frequently had none but persons interested in his will about him during his sickness, peculiarly liable to fraud. Jacobs' *Law Dict.*, *sub voc. Nuncupative Will*, *cf.* Gabrielis Vazquez, *de Testamentis*, cap. i. vj. in *Opuscula Moralia*, Lugd. 1631, p. 238.

l. 726. Abortio vide Benedicti Carpzovii *Rerum Criminalium*, pars i. Quæst. xj. Lipsiæ, 1723, p. 42.

P. 23, l. 728. Listening under walls and windows was a crime at common law. It was one of the duties of a Court Leet Jury to inquire after and present the common drunkard and ale-house haunter, the frequenter of brothels, the common barretor, or strife raiser, "the evesdropper, he that doth hearken under windowes, and the like, to hear and then tell newes to breed debate between neighbours. The night walker, he that sleepeth by day, and walketh by night," and hedge breakers, rogues, vagabonds and sturdy persons, who wander up and down. Sheppard, *Court Keeper's Guide*, p. 48. *Cf.* Scroggs, *Practise of Courts-Leet*, 1714, p. 9. Jacobs' *Complete Court Keeper*, 1731, p. 34. On the 4th of October, 1492, the jury of the manor of Kirton in Lindsey presented that " Will*ielm*us helyfeld Will*ielm*us Chapman sunt co*mmu*nes nyght stalkers tempore incongruo." On the 11th of April of the succeeding year, they further returned that "Joha*nn*es Jonson, husbandman, henr*icus* lucy, Rad*ulph*us Ormesbe; Joha*nn*es hegge, Will*ielm*us helyfeld, R*ic*ardus Webster sunt co*mmu*nes nyght stalkers & ewys droppers tempore incongruo in nocte."— *Rot. Cur.*

l. 743. Chrismatories and fonts were ordered to be kept securely locked, for fear that weak or evil disposed persons should resort to the holy oils or consecrated water for magical purposes. Hart's *Eccl. Records*, 204.

l. 740. When the *child of Bristow* saw his father suffering the agonies of purgatorial fire,

"'Fader,' he said, 'y charge yow tel me,
what is moste ayens the,
and doth yow most disese.'
'Tethynges and offrynges sone,' he sayd,
'for y them never truly payd,
wherfor my peynes may not cesse;
but if it be restored agayn
to as many churches in certayne,
and also mykel encresse.'
—*Harl. MS.* 2382, fol. 118, in *Retrosp. Rev.* 1854, p. 205.

l. 741. If it were known that blood had been shed in a church or churchyard, or if murder or adultery had been committed therein, the place so defiled required reconciliation by the bishop. See several forms for this purpose in Martene, *De Antiq. Eccl. Rit.* ij. 285.

l. 744. *Departyng* = Death. This very beautiful and reverent mode of speaking of our passage from the phenomenal world to the realities beyond was once not uncommon.

[1552]. "I gyve and bequeathe to the Lady Jane, my wyffe, all my stuffe of household that shall fortune to be here in my house in or neere London at the tyme of my *departure*."—*Will of Tho. Wriothesley, Earl of Southampton*, in *Trevelyan Papers*, i. 207.

[1566]. "One alter stone sold to Will*ia*m Thixton, and he caused yt to be laide on his grave when he *departed*."—*Monumenta Superstitionis* in Peacock's *Ch. Furniture*, 121.

Around a stone bearing the arms of Scott of Bucclugh, in one of the outer walls of Branxholme Tower is inscribed :—

"Sir Wl. Scott, of Branxheim, Knyt, yoe of Sir William Scott, of Kirkurd, Knyt, began ye work upon ye 24 of Marche, 1571, ye'r quha departit at Gods pleasure ye 17 April, 1574."—Scott's *Border Antiq.* ij. 103.

P. 24, l. 766. Angels are usually divided into nine orders, viz. Seraphims, Cherubims, Thrones, Dominions, Principalities, Powers, Virtues, Archangels, and Angels. The germ of this classification is to be found in St. Paul, *Eph.* i. 21; *Col.* i. 16. Butler's *Lives of Saints*, May, viij.

Protestant writers have commonly computed but seven orders. They leave out Principalities and Virtues. Bradford's *Writings*, i. 274, 338, 341. Bull's *Christian Prayers*, 108. There has always, however, been much difference of opinion on the question. For curious information of the legendary sort, see Thomas Heywood's *Hierarchy of the blessed Angels*, fol. 1635.

l. 784. "Item excommunicati sunt ab omnibus archiepiscopis et episcopis Angliæ omnes, qui veniunt aut faciunt contra magnam chartam Angliæ, quae sententia est per sedem apostolicam pluries confirmata." *Constitutiones*, Joh. Peckham, archiepisc. Cant. A.D. 1281. Wilkins, *Conc.* ii. 57.

The form of greater excommunication, reprinted by Mr. Maskell from the Sarum Manual of 1530, contains a passage similar to the above, but more explicit.

"Also tho that breke any point of the kinges great chartre, or chartre of the forest, in wiche chartre is writen the fredoms of this lond, that divers kynges have graunted to everi man: in the grete chartre ben xxxv. pointes and the chartre of the forest comprehendith xv pointes; and all archebishops and bishops that longen to england have acursed all tho that broke wytingli any of all these pointes the wych sentence of cursynge hath been often confermed by the court of Rome."—*Mon. Rit.* ii. 299.

Had not the church given the sanction of religion to the first barriers that were set up for the protection of English freedom, we well may doubt whether they or that which they were intended to guard could have resisted the pressure from without.

P. 26, l. 845. *Flotterer*, a ship-man, a sailor. A.S. *Flota*, a ship; *Flot-here*, a body of seamen; *Flot-mann*, a sailor. Low. Ger. *Flote*, a raft. Fr. *Flotte*, a fleet. *Flotson* or *Flotsam* "is when a ship is drowned or othewise perished, & the goods float vpon the sea, & they are giuen to the Lord Admirall by his letters patents," *Les Termes de la Ley. cf.* Cowell's *Dict. sub voc. Flote*-grass or *Flotter*-grass, gramen fluviatile, so called because it floats upon the water. Skinner, *Etymolog. sub voc.* Prompt. Parv. i. 168. Gerarde's *Herbal*, 1636, p. 14. In Lincolnshire we now call this weed Wreck.

P. 27, l. 878. Certain chapels and monasteries of royal foundation were exempt from ordinary jurisdiction. The authorities of these places were responsible for their acts to Rome only, and the priests therein were permitted, as an especial privilege, to celebrate marriages and hear the confessions of persons who were unconnected with the establishments. Battle Abbey, Waltham Abbey, the priory of St. Oswald of Nostell, Co. York, and St. Martin's Church, London, were privileged places. See du Fresne, *Gloss. sub voc. Capella*.

l. 894. *Wlatyng*, loathing, disgust. A.S. *Wlætung*, *wlatung*.

"Vorzoþe and zuo heþ god grat wlatiynge to ham þet ine þese þinges habbeþ blisse."—*Ayenbite of Inwyt*, 216.

P. 28, l. 907. *Fulhelt*, most probably. *Helt* in the dialects of Lancashire means likely, probable, perhaps. Halliw. *Dict.* O.N. *helzt*. Dan. *helst*, mostly in a high degree, most frequently, superlative of *heldr*, rather.

P. 29, l. 939. When our Lord was represented as Judge, the instincts of the mediæval artists told them that it was fitting that they should show the wounds in his sacred hands and feet. Most churches had in them, either frescoed on the walls, carved in stone, or stained in the windows, a picture of the doom. It was one of the commonest sights that met the eyes of the men and women of the Middle Ages, and thus

"hys woundys fresche and rede,"

the tokens of His boundless love, became also the symbols of His justice. Violence and neglect have deprived us of nearly all these outward manifestations of our fathers piety and faith. Where it has been attempted to replace them, the old childlike and mystic spirit has been usually wanting.

Perhaps the grandest representation of the Lord Jesus as Judge which the world possesses, is the figure painted by Orcagna in the Campo Santo of Pisa. He is seated upon a rainbow within an ovoïdal aureole, clad in sumptuous vestments with a tiara—as the sign of the highest spiritual sovereignty upon his brows. The attitude of the figure is pacific and benevolent, but of terrible majesty. The right hand, the sign of power, is raised not in menace, but in love, to show the print of the nail in its palm; with the left—the hand of mercy— He draws away his robe to show the cruel spear-stab in his side. The skirts of the garment are so arranged as to reveal a part—not the whole—of the wound in each foot.

P. 30, l. 974.

" She is abused, stolen from me and corrupted,
By spells and medicines bought of mountebanks."
—*Othello*, i. 3.

Drinks to enforce lechery have been in use from the most remote recorded antiquity to the present time. See Burton's *Anat. Mel.* Pt. iii. *Sc.* 2, *Memb.* iii. *Subst.* 5, and the numberless books he quotes. See also Horsts, *Zauber Bibliothec*, and Colin de Plancy, *Dict. Infernale*. Newton, in his *Tryall of a man's owne selfe*, 12mo. Lond. 1602, p. 116, as quoted in Ellis's Brand's *Antiq.* ij. 603, asks, under the head of breaches of the seventh commandment, whether "By any secret sleight, or cunning, as Drinkes, Drugges, Medicines, charmed Potions, Amatorious Philters, figures, characters, or any such like paltering Instruments, Devices, or Practises, thou hast gone about to procure others to doate for love of thee." This seems to be little more than a quotation from some Catholic book of examinations for confession.

These charms were not intended to procure sexual love alone. There is a shocking case on record of a Miss Mary Blandy, the daughter of a solicitor at Henley-on-Thames, who in the year 1751 was the cause of her father's death by giving to him a certain white powder—most probably arsenic—which her lover, a certain Captain William Henry Cranstoun, had sent her for that purpose, making her believe that it was a love-potion, and that its effect would be to make Mr. Blandy favourable to Cranstoun's addresses to his daughter. The poor woman was tried for murder in the Divinity School at Oxford, on the 9th of March, 1752, and hanged on the Castle-green on the 6th of

April following.—*Gent. Mag.* xxi. 376, 486; xxij. 108, 116, 152, 188. There is a list of the pamphlets relating to this horrible case in Bohn's Loundes' *Bibl. Manual.*

P. 32, l. 1046. *Kynde,* semen.—Chaucer, *Parson's Tale,* ed. Morris, iij. 355.

l. 1054. *Hele,* hide, cover, conceal. A.S. *Hélan.*

> "And *helud* shal ben wiþ a cloþ."
> —*Signs of Death in Polit. Relig. and Love Poems,* p. 224, l. 2.

"Be it made to him a cloþe þat he is *helid* wiþ, and as belt þat is he ai gird wiþ."—Wicliffe's [?] *Lollard Doctrines,* Camd. Soc. p. 24.

[1473] "ij. kerchyvys for to *hele* the sacrament."—Boy's *Sandwich,* 374.

P. 35, l. 1145. Our ancestors, like children, delighted in bright and strongly contrasted colours. Party-coloured garments were very common. They frequently, though not always, had an heraldic signification. In some highly interesting illuminations representing the Courts of Law of the time of Henry VI., published by the late Mr. Corner, in the *Archæologia,* v. 39, p. 357, the serjeants and most of the officials are represented in party-coloured robes. When Charles first Duke of Manchester went as ambassador to Venice [1696 or 1707], his servants wore liveries of this kind. What was once an honourable costume became in time, by a process of degradation well known to antiquaries, the badge of a degrading office. In quite modern days the executioner at Palermo was clad, when on duty, in a party-coloured dress of red and yellow.—*Ibid.* 372.

P. 36, l. 1174. *Drawe on tret,* drawn out, drawn at length, come to a point. I have not met with the phrase elsewhere.

P. 39, l. 1287. *Wedde,* a pledge. A.S. *Wed* (from Goth. *With-an,* to join, to bind). Dut. *Wedde.* Belg. *Wedden.* Hence *Wed,* to marry. *Wedding, Wedlock. Wedbedrip,* the customary service under-tenants paid to their lords in cutting corn and other harvest works.

"1325. Robertus Filius Nicholai Germayn tenet unum messuagium & dimidiam virgatam in bondagio ad voluntatem Domini & debet unam aruram in Yeme & unam sarculaturam & debet *Wedbedrip* pro voluntate Domini."—*Paroch. Antiquit.* 401 in Cowel, *sub voc.*

Wadset, a mortgage. A Scottish law term. Sandford's *Treatise on Entails in Scotl.* 262.

P. 41, l. 1328. All men were not bound to fast to the same degree, or in the same manner. The fasts of the monastic orders were harder to bear than those of lay people, and the monks differed much among themselves in the severity, order, and frequency of their fasts. Each diocese had its own rules, so that it sometimes happened that the dwellers on one side of a street were merrily feasting, while those on the other were mortifying themselves on fish. This was the case in Cheapside, in the sixteenth century, where one row of the houses happened to be in the diocese of Canterbury, and the opposite one in that of London (Pilkington's *Works, Parker Soc.*, 557). Bishops had authority in their respective dioceses to grant dispensations from all fasts. The Crown seems to have exercised a co-ordinate jurisdiction. Several licences not to fast may be found on the Patent Rolls, and memoranda relating to the same order of things may be found in many other places among our public records, *e.g.* in 1222 or 1223, John the son of Henry was indebted to the king in four marks "pro licentia comedendi," half of which sum he had paid into the treasury, and the rest was still owing (*Mag. Rot.* 7, *II.* 3, *Rot.* 11, *a. Everw.* as quoted in Madox, *Hist. Exchequer*, 1711, p. 353). Licences of this sort continued to be in use long after the Reformation; one dated 9th February, 1580-1, is preserved, by which the Archbishop of Canterbury, Edmund Grindal, permits Sir Edward Verney, of Penley, Knight, to eat flesh on days forbidden, for the term of his life, on the ground that a diet of fish disagreed with him; he received also the additional favour of being permitted to share these pleasures of the table with his wife and any three other persons whom he might select (*Verney Papers*, 85). A similar licence, by Thomas Westfield, S.T.D., rector of the church of St. Bartholomew the Great, London, granted in the year 1639 to Mrs. Mary Anthony, wife of John Anthony, of the same parish, Doctor of "Phisick," was printed at length in the *Gentleman's Magazine* for April, 1812, p. 314. The churchwardens of this parish received on behalf of the poor for licences such as these i*l.* vj*s.* viij*d.* from noblemen, and vj*s.* viij*d.* from those of lower degree. In Scotland it would seem that after the Reformation these licences were granted by the civil power, without even a pretence of ecclesiastical authority.—*Ibid.* p. 24.

P. 41, l. 1352. *Sybbe*, akin. A.S. *Sib, Gesibb.*

"A woman may in no lesse sinne assemble with her *Godsib*, than with her own fleshly father."—Chaucer, *Parson's Tale; De luxuria.*

"A Stuarts are na' *sib* to the king."
—Scottish Proverb, Ramsay's *Scottish Life and Charac.* p. 145.

"By the religion of our holy church they are ower *sibb* thegither."—*Antiquary*, ch. xxxiii.

The word is still used in Lincolnshire, *e.g.* "our Marmaduke is *sib* to all the gentles in the country, though he has come down to lead coals."—*Circa*, 1856.

l. 1355. *Ankeras,* a female ankret. The ankrets were persons bound by vows to lead a solitary life. They usually dwelt in the church, sometimes in a little lodge adjoining. Their duty when in holy orders was to say mass, evensong, etc., and to assist the parochial clergy; probably also to clean the sacred vessels, and take care of the church furniture. The duties of the ankress were much the same as those of the ankret who was not in holy orders. She sometimes, though it would seem more rarely, lived within the church. In 1383 William de Belay, of Lincoln, left to an ankress named Isabella, who dwelt in the church of the Holy Trinity, in Wigford, within the city of Lincoln, 13*s.* 4*d.* In 1391 John de Sutton left her 20*s*; in 1394 John de Ramsay left her 12*d.* Besides these she had numerous other legacies from dying citizens, who at that awful crisis were reminded, most touchingly, perhaps, by the severe mortification of one whom they had almost daily before their eyes of the higher life and narrower way which they in health and prosperity had shrunk from or forgotten. In 1453 an ankress named Matilda supplied the place of Isabella, who, we may suppose, had long since gone to her reward. In that year John Tilney, one of the Tilneys of Boston (See ped. in Thompson's *Hist*. 373), left "Domine Matilde incluse infra ecclesiam Sancte Trinitatis ad gressus in civitate Lincoln, vj*s.* viij*d.*" In 1502 Master John Watson, a chaplain [capellanus] in Master Robert Flemyng's Chantry, left xij*d.* to the ankers [ankress?] at the Greese Foot. This church of the Holy Trinity, "ad gressus," seems to have been for a long period the abode of a female recluse. It was called "ad gressus" on account of standing at the bottom of the steep flight of stairs by which men ascended from the lower to the higher city. A street or highway, called the New-road, now passes over the once hallowed spot. The remains of those who slept within its inclosure have, I believe, been dispersed. The steps from which the church took its name are now named the Greecen or Greetstone Stairs. In Norfolk stairs are called *grissens*. I am informed they are still spoken of as *grices* in Lincolnshire, but have myself never heard the word. It was not obsolete here in 1566.

"The steers or *gryses* coming vpp to the altare."
—*Mon. Sup. Folkingham*, in Peacock's *Ch. Fur.* 81.

John Haster, a goldsmith, kept a shop at "the mynster gresses," at York, in 1510. He was presented at the visitation for having suspicious persons in his house at "unconvenient tymes."—*Detecta Quædam in Visitat. Ebor.* Surtees' Soc. 35, p. 262.

Thomas Hearne has printed an episcopal commission, dated 1402, for shutting up John Cherde, a monk of Ford Abbey. Trokelowe's *Annals*, 263. It would seem that an episcopal licence was necessary ere a man or woman could assume this manner of life. Richard Francis, an ankret, is spoken of as "inter quatuor parietes pro Christo inclusus."—Langt. *Chron.* ij. 625.

P. 42, l. 1365. *Clyppinge*, embracing, hence cutting. A.S. *Clyppan*, to embrace.

"Quaþ blauncheflur ich com anon,
Ac floriz *cleppen* here bigon."
—*Floris and Blanchf.* 67, 594.

"To *clippen* & kissen they counten in tounes,
The damoseles that to the daunce sewe."
—*Plowman's Tale*, Edit. 1687, p. 165.

A Lincolnshire peasant said to the editor, concerning one of her neighbours, that "She *clipped* and cuddled the bairn as thof she'd never seen it sin Candlemas." We still talk here of sheep clipping for sheep shearing.

P. 45, l. 1458. The holy-bread, the holy-loaf, or eulogia, was ordinary leavened bread cut into small pieces, blessed, and given to the people after mass was over. The idea entertained by some persons at the period of the Reformation, and in subsequent times, that this rite was instituted as a substitute for the Holy Communion is erroneous. Modern writers have sometimes even confounded the two. Holy bread had nothing sacramental in its nature: it was used in the manner of the ancient love-feasts as a type of the Christian fellowship that should exist among those who were of the household of faith. This practise was once almost universal in Western Christendom, and prevailed to some extent among the Greeks, where it was called Ἀντίδωρα. It has now gone entirely out of use in this country. I believe, however, it is still distributed in some of the dioceses of France. Thomas Becon, Archbishop Cranmer's chaplain, speaks of it in his catechism. He says that "because the people should not be altogether without some outward thing to put them in remembrance of the body-breaking and blood-shedding of Christ, the Papists have brought into the Church two ceremonies, that is to say, *holy-bread* and holy-water; and they every Sunday minister them to the common people instead of the honourable sacrament of the body and blood of Christ, by giving them the bread to eat, and by casting the water on their faces." It was customary in early times for the receivers to carry home this "panis benedictus." It was said that in the fifteenth century some people used to employ it as a charm, and on that account carry it about their persons. One of Cranmer's articles of enquiry, published in the second year of Edward VI., is "whether any person hath abused the ceremonies, as in casting holy water upon his bed, or bearing about him *holy bread*, St. John's Gospel, ringing of holy bells, or keeping of private holy days, as tailors, bakers, brewers, smiths, shoemakers, and such other."

One of the demands of the Devonshire men, who, in 1549, rose in arms to fight for the restoration of the old religion, was that they might "have *holy-bread* and holy-water every Sunday." The martyrologist Foxe gives us the words which Hugh Latimer was wont to use when he distributed the holy loaf to his flock:—

> "Of Christ's body this is the token,
> Which on the cross for your sins was broken;
> Wherefore of your sins you must be forsakers,
> If of Christ's death ye will be partakers."

It was decreed by the Constitutions of Giles de Bridport, Bishop of Salisbury, A.D. 1254, that the parishioners should provide the holy loaf every Sunday. The order in which it was provided in the parish of Stanford-in-the-Vale, Co. Berks., may be seen from an extract from the church account book of that parish, published by Dr. Rock.

There were "ij. *hally-brede* basckatts" among the goods belonging to St. Olave's, Southwark, in 1558. In 1566, at Gonwarby, in Lincolnshire, "one *hally bred* skeppe [was] sold to Mr. Allen, and he maketh a baskett to carrie ffishe in."

In the Sacristy of St. Andrew, at Vercelli, is still preserved a curious knife with a box-wood handle, carved with the occupations of each month of the year. This instrument is thought to have been intended for cutting the blessed bread. It has an additional interest to Englishmen from the fact that it is believed to have once belonged to St. Thomas of Canterbury. Bingham's *Antiq.* ed. 1834, v. 300, 322. Rock's *Ch. of our Fathers*, i. 135-140. Becon's *Catech.* ed. 1844, 260. Cranmer's *Works*, ed. Fox, ii. 158, 503. Wilkins' *Conc.* i. 714. Peacock's *Ch. Fur.* 86, 96. *Gent. Mag.* 1837, i. 492. Hart's *Eccl. Records*, 205, 294.

l. 1465. *Lychwake.* A.S. *lic*, a body; *wæccan*, to watch. The Lake-wake or Lyke-wake was the watching of the corpse, common among all simple-minded people. It arose out of some of the holiest instincts of our nature, but has at all times been liable to foul corruption. We have ample evidence that these death watchings often degenerated in the Middle Ages into riotous festivals. The custom is not extinct in Ireland, Scotland, or Sweden. I believe it still lingers in the Northern Shires of England. John Aubrey has preserved in his *Remains of Gentilismo & Judaisme*, Lansd. MS. 231, fol. 114, an account of these festivous funeral rites taken from the lips of "Mr. Mawtese, in whose fathers youth sc*ilicet* about 60 yeares since [1686 now] at country vulgar Funeralls was sung this song."

"At the Funeralls in Yorkshire to this day they continue the custome of watching & sitting vp all night till the Body is interred. In the interim some kneel downe and pray (by the corps), some play at cards, some drink & take Tobacco: they have also Mimicall playes & sports, *e.g.* they choose a simple young fellow to be a Judge, then the Suppliants (having first blacked their they play likewise hands by rubbing it under the bottome of the Pott) at Hott-cockles. beseech his Lo*rdshi*p and smutt all his face.

. . . . .

The beleefe in Yorkshire was amongst the vulgar (& p*er*haps is in part still) that after the parsons death, the Soule went over Whinnimore, and till about $\frac{1624}{1616}$ at the Funerall a woman came [like a Præfica], and sung the following Song :—

This ean night, this ean night,
eve[r]y night and awle

NOTES. 91

  Fire and Fleet[1] and Candle-light,   [1] water.
    and Christe recieve thy Sawle.
  When thou from hence doest pass away,
    every night and awle,
  To Whinny-moore thou comest at last,
    and Christ recieve thy[2] Sawle.   [2] 'silly, poor,' *inter-lined.*
  If ever thou gave either hosen or shuu,
    every night and awle.
  Sitt thee downe and putt them on,
    and Christ recieve thy Sawle.
  But if hosen nor shoon thou never gave nean,
    every night, etc.
  The Whinnes[3] shall prick thee to the bare beane,   [3] Furze.
    and Christ recieve thy Sawle.
  From Whinny-moor that thou mayst pass,
    every night, etc.
  To Brig o' Dread, thou comest at last,
    and Christ, etc.,
    no brader than a thread.   [fol. 114 b.]
  From Brig of Dread that thou mayst pass,
    every night, etc.
  To Purgatory fire thou com'st at last,
    and Christ, etc.
  If ever thou gave either Milke or drinke,
    every night, etc.
  The fire shall never make thee shrink,
    and Christ, etc.
  But if milk nor drink thou never gave nean,
    every night, etc.
  The Fire shall burn thee to the bare bene,
    and Christ recieve thy Sawle.

A version of this strange dirge, varying in a few minute particulars, was printed by Sir Walter Scott, in his *Minstrelsy of the Scottish Border* (Edit. 1861, ii. 135-142). I should have imagined that it had been derived from the same MS. as the above, had not Sir Walter spoken of it in such a manner as to induce us to believe that it was still the custom to sing it at funerals when he made his great collection of oral poetry. His words are—" This is a sort of charm sung by the lower ranks of Roman Catholics in some parts of the north of England, while watching a dead body previous to interment. The tune is doleful and monotonous, and joined to the mysterious import of the words has a solemn effect."

It is possible that these verses may yet linger as a tradition among the peasantry of the North of England. If so, it is much to be desired another copy should be procured. The above is evidently corrupted in several places.

In an account of some matters relating to the neighbourhood of

Gisborough, written about the end of the sixteenth century by a correspondent of Sir Thomas Challoner, who signed himself H. Tr . . . . . we have the following curious picture. There cannot be much doubt that the "songe" which "certaine women singe," was of the same nature if not identical with the verses preserved by John Aubrey.

"When any dieth certaine women singe a songe to the dead body, recytinge the iorney that the p*a*rtie deceased must goe, and they are of beleife (such is their fondnesse) that once in their liues y*t* is good to giue a payre of newe shoes to a poore man, forasmuch as after this life they are to passe barefoote through a greate launde full of thornes & furzen, excepte by the meryte of the Almes aforesaide, they have redemed their forfeyte: for at the edge of the launde an aulde man shall meete them w*i*th the same shoes that were giuen by the p*a*rtie when he was liuinge, and after he hath shodde them he dismisseth them to goe through thicke and thin w*i*thout scratch or scalle."— Cotton MS. *Julius*, F. vi. fol. 438 *b*.

P. 46, l. 1503.

> "Now turn again, turn again, said the Pinder,
> For a wrong way you have gone, &c.,
> For you have forsaken the kings highway,
> And made a path over the corn," &c.
> —*The Pinder of Wakefield & Robin Hood.*

There was in former days a very strong feeling of dislike against those persons who trod down growing corn. The sentiment was more intense than the mere money loss warranted. In times when famines were probable contingencies, people realized more fully than they do now the wickedness of destroying human food. The feeling has happily not as yet died out among our rural poor.

P. 48, l. 1497. The ecclesiastical councils of Christendom have frequently prohibited unclean beasts being allowed to feed in churchyards. In some parts of Denmark the intrusion of cattle in graveyards is prevented by an iron grating being fixed in the gateway, under which a deep hole has been excavated. Over this men and women can walk with ease, but sheep and pigs are unable to do so as their feet slip between the bars. Hamilton's *Sixteen Months in the Danish Isles*, i. 135.

P. 51, l. 1658. *Quede*, wicked = the devil. Dutch, *Quade*, evil.

> "He so haveth of fur mest, he schal beo smal and red,
> other blak with crips her, lene, and somdel *qued*."
> —*Pop. Treatises on Science*, 138.

> "And lete me neuere falle
> In boondis to the *queed*."
> —*Hymns to Virg. and Christ*, p. 6, l. 18.

l. 1671. Dead men's bones, corpses in process of decay, worms devouring putrid bodies, and similar subjects, were objects of frequent contemplation to our forefathers. The abbots of the Carthusian order, when in chapter, had a human skull laid before them. Many mediæval monuments survive where the deceased is represented as an emaciated corpse or a fleshless skeleton. See *Notes and Queries*, 1st series, v. 247, 301, 353, 427, 497; vi. 85, 252, 321, 345, 393, 445, 520; vii 439. Douce's Holbein's *Dance of Death, passim*. Shakespere had evidently been deeply affected by suchlike objects of contemplation.

P. 53, l. 1719. This shows that the author took it for granted that there would be in every church a sanctus bell, which would be rung to turn men's thoughts to God at the moment of consecration.

P. 54, l. 1763. ʒop, wary. A.S. *Geap*, crooked, deceitful, cunning.

"He stiȝtleȝ stif in stalle
Ful ȝep in þat nw zere."
—*Sir Gawayne and the Green Knight*, p. 4, l. 104.

P. 58, l. 1872. *Hull*, cover. A.S. *Hélan*. The act of shelling beans or peas, or removing the outer husk of walnuts, is called *hulling* in Lincolnshire. Pods or husks are *hulls*.

P. 59, l. 1937. *Coppe*, a spider. A.S. *Attercoppa*, literally a poison head, cup, or bug. Cobweb is a corruption of coppe-web. There is a wonderful tale in the preface to Hearne's Langloft's *Chron*. p. cc., of three persons being poisoned by the venom of an *atturcoppe*, of whom two died, and the third was so near death that he made his will, and in all other ways got ready for his departure, when, happening to think of Saint Winefrede and of the miracles wrought by her, he induced his mother to go to her shrine and offer a candle there, and "brynge hym of þe water þat her bones were wasschon yn." With the use of this water he soon recovered, and as a thank-offering he presented at her shrine an image of silver. The account does not say what the image represented. I presume it was a figure either of himself or of the saint who had helped him, perhaps the spider also was shewn.—See *Prompt. Parv. sub roc.* Richardson's *Dict. sub Cobweb.*

GLOSSARIAL INDEX.

	PAGE.	LINE.		PAGE.	LINE.
A-bregge, abridge,	50	1629	Axtree, axletree,	11	334
A-corest, accursed,	26	847	Ay, ever,	14	542
Accursen, accurse,	21	685	Ajte, ought,	48	1556
	24	756			
A-ferd, frightened. Still used in North Lincolnshire,	44	1447	Backbyte, backbiting,	39	1267
			Baldely, plainly,	35	1132
			Basclard, a dagger,	2	48
Agen, against,	22	715	Bawdryke, a belt,	2	48
A-go, gone,	38	1252	Be-bled, blodied,	59	1934
	47	1526	Beleue, belief,	12	366
Al-gate, anyhow, always,	48	1560	Ben, be,	16	526
	58	1878	Benefyces, benefits,	10	317
Als, as,	13	394	Bere, noise, uproar,	8	240
	32	1055		9. 276,	289
A-bygge, abide,	61	2010	Beren, bear,	21	688
Amendment,	25	760	Be-stad, bestood, circumstanced,	45	1474
An-elet, anointed,	56	1812			
Annoynted,	21	670	Bete, make better = heal, save, cure,	16	515
A-nont, upon,	60	1961			
Ankeras, Ankress, Anchoress, a female hermit,	41	1355	Beth, be,	1	6
	48	1559	Bicquest,	23	746
			Bifor, before,	16	
A-pert, openly,	44	1448	Billes,	22	709
Arrours, errors,	63		Blyue, quickly,	13	394
Artykele, article,	14	458		43	1418
Aster, Easter,	5	143	Bollyng, bull baiting,	11 n.	
	8	241	Bondes,	21	663
At ene, at once,	3	82	Boo, both,	1	3
A-tent, intent,	29	952	Bordes, jests, games,	9	267
Auter, altar,	57	1867		18	588
A-vys, advice,	8	226		40	1325
A-vow, A-voue, vow,	13	396	Boren, born,	23	726

GLOSSARIAL INDEX.

	PAGE.	LINE.
Brenne, burn,	4	116
	21	668
Brenner, burner,	54	1767
Busshelles,	22	711
But, except,	23	738
By-dene, presently, at once,	58	1870
By-forn, before,	16	519
By-gylet, beguiled,	40	1299
Byspyng, bishoping = confirmation,	20	646
By-taghte, taught,	48	1580
By-twynne, between,	7	220
Candell,	24	777
	58	1875
Canons,	24	769
Caste,	36	1182
Casteth, plots, contrives,	49	1595
Castynge, vomiting,	61	2000
Chafare, merchandize, exchange, barter. A.S. *ceáp*, a bargain. Hence the family name *Chaffers*,	40	1299
Chames, charms, spells,	12	368
Charmes,	23	734
Chartor of fforest,	24	784
Chartors, charters,	23	732
Chast, chaste,	2	21
Chaunge, change,	20	638
Chost, strife,	11	338
	45	1477
Churchay, churchyard. A.S. *cyrice*, church. *Heg*, hay, grass, or *hege*, a hedge or fence,	11 *n*. 23 *n*.	
Chyrche, church,	16	527
Clanseþ, cleanseth,	17	528
Clyppyng, embracing = cutting, clipping,	42	1365
Cloystrere, cloisterer = monk, canon,	47	1523
Comyn, common,	23	748
Comyn wommon, harlot,	41	1358
Confermynge,	17	529
Conne, know,	1	16
Consenten,	22	693
Connynge, knowing,	46	1512
Consentoures, consentors,	22	721
Contrycyone,	50	1624
Coppe, spider. A.S. *attercoppa*, a spider, *lit.* a poison head, poison bag, or poison cup,	59	1937
Corne,	22	721
Corporas, a linen cloth used in the service of the mass,	59	1922
Cosynage, cousinhood, relationship,	6	168
Cotteyng, quoiting, playing at quoits,	11 *n*.	
Couetyse, covetousness,	39	1281
Counter, contrary,	51	1665
Court,	27	877
Couth, known,	27 *n*.	
Cowþe, could,	19	619
Cowpulle, copulation,	7	194
Creawnce, credence,	55	1788
Creme, holy oil,	18.	582, 634
Cristendom,	23	725
Crome, crumb,	62	2013
Croys, cross,	14	437
Crysme, holy oil,	18	582
Cunnen, can,	8	237
Cuppes,	22	712
Curatowre, curate,	31	1023
Dampne, damn,	25	758
Dawe, days,	1	5
Ded, death,	8	247
Deden, did,	17	556
Dedeyn, disdain,	35	1159
Dedlyche, deadly,	33	1081
Defendant,	23	738
Defoulen, defile, pollute,	23	741
Dele, part,	16	499
Deme, sentence,	16	523
Departen, separate,	24	756
Departyng, departure = death,	23	746

	PAGE.	LINE.
Derrer, dearer,	12	383
Despuyte, dispute,	21	673
Destroyen,	22	692
Destruye, destroy,	38	1240
Deuors, divorce,	7	197
Diffame,	22	707
Disapules, disciples,	24	768
Distroubleth, troubleth,	22	717
Domes-day,	16	521
Drawe on tret,	36	1173
Droken, drunken,	20	631
Dronkelee, Dronkelewe, drunkenness,	2	31
Dronken,	19	623
Dryʒt, the Lord Jesus Christ. A.S. *drihten*,	14	426
Dyuynyte,	14	456
Dyʒte, dispose = deck, adorn. A.S. *dihtan*,	57	1867
Eghþe, eighth,	{16 / 21}	{497 / 665}
Eine, even,	22	705
Eke, also,	9	275
Elde, age,	8	236
Ellen, ells,	22	713
Ellus, else,	48	1556
Elyng, healing,	17	533
Enchewe, eschew,	2	28
Ensaumpul, ensample,	{15 / 22}	{472 / 703}
Enuyet, envied,	38	1229
Eschewe,	20	637
Euenyng, equal,	38	1229
Executores,	23	944
Experimentes,	23	733
Eyres, heirs,	23	732
Eysel, vinegar, A.S. *Eisile*,	58	1884
Fabul, Fable,	18	578
Falsen, make false, forge,	22	709
Fanoun, a maniple, one of the vestments worn by the priest at mass,	59	1917
Fare, go,	9	265

	PAGE.	LINE.
Fare, proceeding, custom,	11	332
Faren, go,	1	5
Fay, faith,	12	362
Fayre, go,	25	816
Fel, } sharp, Fell, }	{46 / 24}	{1513 / 781}
Fende, fiend,	12	370
Ferde, fear,	20	635
Fere, undaunted. Dan. *För*. O.N. *Færr*,	13	407
Fere, fellowship,	2	25
Fere, companion = wife,	6	190
Ferus, companion,	48	1569
Fey, faith,	14	453
Feynet, feigned,	34	1101
Feyntyse, faintness,	37	1207
Feyre, fair,	9	280
Fir, for,	21	681
Flette, flat = floor,	9	273
Flotterer, a ship-man, a sailor,	26	845
Folyly, foolishly,	44	1439
Folghthe, baptism,	{5 / 17}	{149 / 528}
Folowe, baptise,	3	85
Folwynge, baptism. A.S. *Fulluht*,	5	146
Fondyng, trial, temptation,	13	420
Fonne, a fool,	12	358
Fore-done, destroy,	2	44
For-lore, lost,	10	299
For-slowthed, lost by sloth,	64	
Forswore,	30	977
For-ʒeueth, forgiveth,	10	321
Fott-ball,	11	*n.*
Frechedly, freshly,	41	1382
Fremd, stranger. A.S. *fremed*, foreign,	{41 / 48}	{1322 / 1558}
Frerus, Freres = friars,	48	1570
Freyne, ask,	28	911
Frutes,	22	721
Fulhelt,	28	906
Fyted, fitted = well fitting, or, perhaps, well matched as to diversity of colour,	35	1146

GLOSSARIAL INDEX.

	PAGE.	LINE.
Fyʒte, fight,	26	850
Galones, gallons,	22	711
Gart, caused,	12	366
Gnede, grudge. A.S. *gneadlicnes*, frugality, temperance,	10	319
Glotorye, gluttony,	{ 40	1313
	{ 52	1705
Godhede,	16	510
Goth, goeth,	51	1682
Grame, anger. A.S. *gram*, angry,	30	967
Grede, greedy. A.S. *grǽdig*,	10 *n.*	
Gret, grieved. A.S. *grǽtan*, to weep,	36	1173
Greuus, grievous,	12	374
Greythe, readily, speedily,	{ 11	346
	{ 18	587
Grope, feel = investigate,	28	911
Gruchynge, grudging,	37	1219
Grylle, sorrowful, fearful,	{ 4	103
	{ 24	780
Grym,	48	1560
Gryth, protection,	52	1693
Gult, trespass, guilt,	{ 13	419
	{ 34	1099
Gulty, guilty,	28	900
Hale, secret, concealment. A.S. *hélan*,	42	1384
Hallowen,	23	755
Halybred, the holy bread, *eulogia*,	45	1458
Halydawes, holydays,	7	203
Hand-ball, a game,	11 *n.*	
Haunce, enhance,	53 *n.*	
Hele, hell,	12	369
Hele, hide, cover,	{ 16	498
	{ 24	782
	{ 46	1507
	{ 49	1592
Helet, held,	32	1053
Helle, hell,	14	49
Helut, ignorant. A.S. *hélan*,	56	1811

	PAGE.	LINE.
Henne, } hence, hereafter, Hennes, }	{ 53	1735
	{ 10	295
Heo, she,	{ 3	88
	{ 47	1519
Her, their,	22	705
Heremytes, eremites, hermits,	25	770
Heretikes,	22	701
Herinyng, hearing,	22	694
Herre, higher,	47	1527
Herus, hair,	34	1119
Heʒ, high,	50	1631
Heyre, her,	15	490
Hin, in,	23	738
He, she,	7	196
Hodymoke,	62	2031
Hole, whole,	13	407
Holpe, helped,	39	1264
Hond, hand,	23	737
Honde, handiwork,	11	354
Hondweddinge, hand-wedding, an irregular marriage,	7 *n.*	
Hortes, hearts,	24	780
Hosele, to give the holy communion. A.S. *húsl*,	3	82
Hoselet. See Hosele,	8	243
Hoselyng. See Hosele,	8	253
House-breakeres,	23	730
Howsele. See Hosele,	10	294
Howsynge, houses,	35	1147
Hele, cover. A.S. *hélan*,	58	1872
Humanyte,	14	457
Huyde, hide,	34	1105
Huydeth, hideth,	7	201
Huyre, hire, pay, recompense. A.S. *hýr*, hire, wage,	{ 11	354
	{ 30	979
Hyest, hastened,	36	1175
Hyse, his,	{ 14	451
	{ 43	1408
Hyʒt, haste, hurry,	17	559
Iape, a jest,	3	61
I-blende, mixed up,	12	370
I-bore, born,	10	298

GLOSSARIAL INDEX.

	PAGE.	LINE.
I-borste, burst = broken,	30	963
I-bysbed, bishopped, confirmed,	6	158
Idous, hideous. A.S. hydan,	21	679
I-drouk, drunken. Probably here it is the scribe's error for i-do,	40	1295
Iewes,	23	725
I-fere, as companions together,	7	219
I-hoseled. See Hosele,	8	240
Indyscrete,	26	824
I-nome, taken. A.S. niman,	15	495
I-pult, pushed, put,	34	1100
I-queynt, quenched,	37	1194
I-shend, injured,	12	371
I-shende, spoilt,	17	539
I-shent, destroyed,	34	1113
I-shryve, shriven,	8	239
Isenting, consenting,	22	718
I-storbet, disturbed,	45	1459
I-synget, sinned,	40	1313
I-taimed, tempted,	39	1262
I-tened, harmed,	38	1258
Kenne, know, inform,	27	976
	50	1652
	59	1905
Keure, recover,	26	85
Kirk,	16	n.
Knave, boy,	7	217
Knowlache, acknowledge,	28	915
Knowlachynge, acknowledgment,	45	1463
Knylle, knell,	53	1719
Koghe, cough,	27	890
Kore, recover,	26	n.
Kynde, semen,	8	230
	32	1046
Kynde, nature,	7	203
Lafte, left,	21	663
Lask, purge,	53	1736

	PAGE.	LINE
Lasse, less,	33	1068
Laten, Latin,	18	570
Layne, reward,	25	810
	46	1510
Leben, believe,	23	735
Lechery,	47	1548
Lechowre,	43	1394
Ledeth hys lyf, gains his living,	27	871
Lemmon, concubine,	26	830
Lene, lend,	46	1485
Lene, loan,	22	705
Lentenes-day, Easter,	3	75
Lere, teach. A.S. læran,	17	546
Lered, learned = clergy,	38	1258
Lese, lose,	10	325
Lesyng, falsehood,	33	1065
Lette, hinder, hindrance,	21	677
	23	746
Lettres,	22	709
Leue, believe,	9	260
	14	459
Leue, leave,	8	259
Lewd, lay,	20	645
Lewte, loyalty,	31	1024
Leyen, lay,	23	747
Loke, locked,	20	660
Londes, lands,	35	1147
Lone, loan,	12	383
Lyde ȝate, lych gate,	46	1497
Lyet, lied,	33	1065
Lust, list,	25	819
Lutte, light,	51	1659
Luyte, light, little,	39	1268
	43	1416
	53	1747
Luytel, littel,	19	627
Lychwake, the watching of the corpse before burial,	45	1465
Lyth, the body,	42	1365
Madhede, madness,	51	1657
Male, a budget, a satchel = the belly,	41	1343
Malencholy,	39	1269

GLOSSARIAL INDEX.   99

	PAGE.	LINE.
Man-quellers, a destroyer of men, a murderer,	23	730
Matenes, matins,	24	771
May, maid,	41	1351
Mayde,	28	894
Mayn, haste, force,	40	1315
Measures,	22	711
Mede, meed, reward,	24	773
	49	1588
Meyne, company = servant,	37	1196
Meynleyn,	23	732
Mighele, St. Michael,	23	753
Mischawnce, mischance,	62	2011
Mod, mood,	27	883
Mo, more,	17	534
Mon, man,	4	106
Monslaȝt, manslaughter,	47	1535
Mor, more, greater,	22	706
Mot, much,	48	1578
Mowe, may,	4	95
	21	682
Myche, much,	25	791
Mynge, mingle = mind, remember, observe. A.S. *mengian*,	48	1555
	62	2027
Mynne, remember,	8	233
	17	529
Myscheueth, unfortunate, ill, happen, an accident,	17	550
Myȝt, mighty,	15	461
Needly, necessarily. *Needlings* is still a Lincolnshire word,	13	401
Negh, nigh,	76	854
Nere, ne were = were not,	19	620
	21	673
Nete, neat = horned cattle,	11	353
Neuer the latter, never the less,	3	87
	8	250
Newe, accrue, come by growth,	11	348
Newed, renewed,	20	642
	48	1575
Neȝ, near,	50	1632
Nome, name,	17	551
	48	1551
Nonne, nun,	41	1355
Nother, Nowþer, } neither,	39	1283
	12	386
Nuye, annoy. O.F. *anoi*, from Lat. *odium*,	4	120
Ny, nor,	18	564
Nym, take = comprehend,	17 *n*.	
Nyste, ignorance. A.S. *nyste*, do not know, from *nitan* (*ne-witan*), not to know,	40	1321
Nythinge, wicked = sparing, niggardly, mean. A.S. *neðing*, a wicked person, an outlaw,	39	1285
Odde weddynge, a private wedding,	7	189
Offeryng,	23	740
Ofyce, office,	20	649
Okere, usury,	12	372
Okereres, usurers,	22	704
On, in,	25	798
On, Ones, } once,	15	465
	20	638
Onlyche, only,	20	656
On rowe, in order,	5	123
	18	560
Ore, grace, mercy,	18	585
Ost, host, the eucharistic bread after consecration,	8	255
Ote, oats,	45	1483
Ouer-dryve, ouer-driven, burdened above what can be borne,	56	1813
Ouer-gate, overmuch, unreasonably,	40	1307
Oyle,	20	634

GLOSSARIAL INDEX.

	PAGE.	LINE.
Oynementes, ointments = the consecrated oils used in baptism, confirmation, extreme unction, etc.	23	734
Oʒt, ought,	51	1657
Parauentur, peradventure,	28	905
Paresche, } parish,	1	17
Parisse, }	21	678
Parsons, persons,	29	928
Party-hosen, parted-hosen, hosen made of diverse colours,	35	1145
Passyngere, passenger,	26	844
Passyone, the Lord's Passion,	14	436
Pay, appease. Fr. *paier*; Lat. *pacere*,	2	34
Pay,	30	989
Person, parson,	22	691
Peyred, impaired,	22	690
Plenere, full. Lat. *plenus*,	14	449
Plungynge,	19	609
Plyʒte, plight,	10	324
Popes,	22	709
Pownce Pylate, Pontius Pilate,	14	434
Poundes,	22	712
Poundrelles,	22	713
Potelles, two-quart measures,	22	712
Pouert, poverty,	35	1134
Poyntes,	24	781
Predycacyon, preaching,	36	1178
Preres, prayers,	24	757
Pris, price,	24	706
Prodder, prouder,	35	1129
Prokeren, procure,	21	689
Proketours, proctors,	22	695
Prow, advantage, profitable. Fr. *prod*,	17	548
	38	1238
	60	1951
Prowde, proud,	34	1127
Pruyde, pride,	34	1107
Putte, pit,	51	1662
Pyked-schone, peaked shoon,	35	1145
Quartes,	22	712
Quede, wicked = the devil,	51	1658
Quyke, alive,	16	523
Raft, stolen, taken off, or away,	21	664
	30	971
Reame, realm,	22	719
Recepetoures, receivers,	22	700
Rede, teach. A.S. *rǽdan*,	1	7
Rede, counsel, advice,	15	481
Rede, red,	29	939
Remyssyone, remission,	14	449
Renabulle, reasonable,	34	1120
Reret, raised up,	38	1243
Reven, spoil,	22	699
Reyng, command,	11	*n.*
Rightvsnesse,	64	
Robben,	22	699
Robbyng,	32	1049
Rowe, row = array, order,	14	447
Roytynge, rioting,	31	998
Ruyflen, ruffling = with rough usage,	22	*n.*
Rybawdye, ribaldry,	3	61
Ryʒt, rightly,	15	460
Sad, gravely, seriously,	9	260
Sakeringe, consecration,	9	285
	10	303
Sarre, sore,	48	1565
Sarrerer, sorer = more excessively, more grievously,	47	1728
Sarazons, Saracens,	23	725
Sawtere, psalter,	2	53
Scales, *misprint* for Seales,	22	709
Schaf, shave,	59	1934
Sched, shed,	32	1046
Scheme, shame,	20	637
Schende, } injure,	50	1646
Schent, }	40	1320

GLOSSARIAL INDEX. 101

	PAGE.	LINE.
Schere þursday, Holy Thursday,	20	638
Scho, she,	4	108
Schonkes, shanks, legs,	27	891
Schrewede, cursed, wicked,	38	1257
Schrewes, wicked persons,	45	1481
Schule, should,	18	587
Schullen, shall,	5	144
Scof,	28	901
Scoler, scholar,	21	844
Seche, seek,	20	651
Seke, sick,	60	1953
Sen, ⎫ see,	1	4
Sene, ⎭	10	327
Sengul, single = unwedded,	7	214
Seyntwary, sanctuary = churchyard,	11	330
Shryffader, shrift-father = confessor,	8	233
Sikerly, securely,	10	n.
Skynnes, kynnes = kind of,	7	210
	50	1638
Sle, ⎫ slay,	2	36
Sleen, ⎭	23	725
Sleer, slayer,	53	1767
Slegh, sly, cunning,	26	855
	46	1513
Sleghþe, sleight,	12	304
Slen, slay,	22	699
Sloghe, slew,	48	1572
Slyly,	17	554
Snel, quick,	4	121
Soccouren,	23	724
Sodenlyche, suddenly,	49	1597
Sofere, suffer,	11	335
Sondes, messages,	56	1838
Sorcery,	30	972
Sotelly, subtilely,	17	n.
Soþe, truth,	16	520
Souke, suck,	59	1923
Soyled, assoiled,	26	848
Spel, ⎫ tale = teaching, doctrine,	6	170
Spelle, ⎭	14	445
	15	482
Spene, spend,	31	1009

	PAGE.	LINE.
Spousayle, wedding,	17	532
Spoyle,	16	509
Spysory, spicery,	44	1433
Stegh, ascended,	16	518
	29	937
Steuene, voice,	13	411
Stoil-ball, a game,	11	n.
Stoke, stuck,	20	n.
Ston,	20	654
Stole, an ecclesiastical vestment,	59	1917
Storbet, disturbed,	36	1168
Stound, a short space of time,	24	778
Straȝt, straitly = strictly,	47	1536
Sturben, disturb,	21	686
Sty, path,	46	1501
Stynteth,	28	896
Suster, sister,	26	830
Swore, oath. A.S. *swerian*,	33	1067
Swinke, labour. A.S. *swinc*,	41	1346
Sybbe, akin. A.S. *sib*, *gesibb*,	26	829
	41	1352
Sych, such,	12	366
Sycurly, securely,	10	317
Sylabul, syllable,	18	577
Symonye,	40	1295
Synes, signs,	61	1985
Synge, Syngen, sin, 33. 1073, 1077		
Syse, seize,	39	1282
Sysourus, jurors, inquest men, assessors,	54	1777
Syȝte, sight,	10	325
Te, to,	26	857
Tele, deceit. A.S. *tæl*, tale, story, fable,	12	368
Telynge, telling = telling fortunes,	12	360
Tenessyng, playing at tennis,	11	n.
Testament,	22	716
Thewes, manners. A.S. *þeaw*,	3	60

GLOSSARIAL INDEX.

	PAGE.	LINE.
Thilk, that same,	10	*n.*
	21	687
Thoght, thought,	18	567
Thryuynge, thriving,	38	1234
Thylke, this,	7	201
Tichen, teaching,	23	737
Tithenges,	22	691
To-fore, before,	7	213
Towayles, towels,	58	1871
Tryste, trust,	34	1126
Tuynde, } shut. A.S.	3	63
Tuynen, } *týnan*,	15	490
Twye, } twice,	4	119
Twyes, }	13	406
Tylle, to,	40	311
þagh, } though,	7	196
þaȝ, }	12	358
þe, thee,	17	552
þenne, than,	25	792
þer-tylle, thereto,	43	1406
þewes, manners,	45	1482
þo, though,	17	535
þoukes, thoughts. A.S.		
þonk, þank,	27	890
þorȝ, through,	15	486
þreteneþe, thirteenth,	16	516
þridde, } third,	16	514
þrydde, }	15	462
þryes, thrice,	13	406
þryfle,	25	806
þrytty, thirty,	62	2016
Vaunce, advance = en-crease,	53	1748
Vche, each,	13	416
Verement, truly,	12	390
	13	403
Verre, very, true,	10	296
Vicary, vicar,	22	691
Vitayles, victuals,	23	724
Vnderlynge, an inferior,	38	1233
Vnholy,	22	723
Vnsware, answer,	29	929
Vnwyse, unwise,	62	2017

	PAGE.	LINE.
Vomyschment, } vomit-	61	2000
Vomysment, } ing,	40	1317
Voys, voice,	34	1117
Vrþe, earth,	15	483
Vsure, usury,	12	372
Vye, envy,	14	435
Vys, advice. Fr. *avis,*	41	1337
Vyse, in sight, in view. Fr. *viser,*	3	66
War, wary,	19	608
Warde, guardianship = able to take care of themselves,	8	236
Warren, curse,	24	756
Wayte, wit = know,	58	1883
Wedde, a pledge, 39.	1287,	1290
Wede, garment,	31	1019
Wededhood, } wedlock,	7	212
Wedhood, }		
Welde, wield = govern, rule,	8	237
Wene, hope = doubt. A.S. *wen,*	12	381
Werkeday,	31	1004
Werne, warn,	26	840
Wetyngly, wittingly,	22	716
Weyletes, cross ways. A.S. *lad;* Sw. *lée,*	23	748
Weynt, done, accomplished,	37	1214
Whad, what,	44	1445
	48	1516
White, wight = quick, active, strong,	34	1022
Whysson-tyde, Whitsuntide. The word is still pronounced thus in Lincolnshire.	5	143
Whatyng, loathing, disgust,	27	893
Wightes, weights,	22	712
Woll, will,	22	714
Wolles, walls,	23	728
Wolþe, will,	5	160

		PAGE.	LINE.
Wonet, wont,		30	980
		39	1265
Wond, fear = hesitate,		12	384
		21	631
		28	904
Worche, work,		53	1718
Worchynge, working,		17	536
Worre, worse,		38	1242
Wote, oats, pronounced *wots* in Lincolnshire,		45 *n.*	
Wowet, wooed,		42	1385
Wrathþed, made angry,		38	1254
Wry, turn away,		27	887
Wrynge, wring,		27	891
Wyndowes,		23	729
Wynnyng,		22	705
Wys, wise,		19	628
Wyte, wit = know,		46	1515
Wytte, knowledge,		8 *n.*	
Wyþ-say, deny, withhold,		39	1292
Wyth-tan, withdrawn, withheld,		40	1297
Wyntynge, witting = knowledge,		13	397
Ydul, idle,		11	356
Yen, eyes,		27	882
Yerdes, yards,		22	713
Yeke, the same. Sc. *ilk*,		10	322
		33	1080
Ypocryse, hypocrisy,		34	1102
Yrke, irk,		16	526
Ys, is,		16	520
Ys, ice,		15	473
ȝaf, gave,		34	1091
ȝates, gates. *Yate* is the Lincolnshire pronunciation,		15	488
ȝef, if,		3	86
ȝen, give,		25	795
ȝerne, earnestly. A.S. *georne*,		2	53
		3	70
ȝerus, years,		53	1738
ȝeue, give,		5	138
ȝeyn-stondynge, against standing = withstanding,		15	491
ȝonge, young,		9	286
ȝop, active,		54	1763
ȝore, sorely,		1	9
		40	1304
ȝow, you,		5	124
		15	470

ADDITIONS AND CORRECTIONS FOR THE SOCIETY'S TEXTS.

[Printed on one side only to allow of each slip being cut off, and gummed in the Text to which it refers.]

12. THE WRIGHT'S CHASTE WIFE.—Page 25, l. 3. *A nun's hen.* Compare—
    She tooke thentertainment of the yong men
    All in daliaunce, *as nice as a nuns hen.*
    Jn. Heywood's Proverbs and Epigrams, 1562, Spenser Society's ed. p.43.
    With the W.C.W., compare the ballad in the British Museum Ballads, 643m.
    "The Fryer Well-fitted; or,
    A Pretty jest that once befel,
    How a maid put a Fryer to cool in the well."
    —Quoted in *Skelton's Works*, ii. 293, ed. Dyce.

14. KYNG HORN, ETC.—Page 58, Cancel side-note to l. 256-60, and read—"No attendants are admitted except eunuchs."
    Gloss *ginne*, l. 258, tool, penis.
    Pref. p. vii. M. Paul Meyer contends, as to the French and English versions of *Horn*,—1. That they are independent of each other. 2. That the French poem represents a more complete state of the legend, and refers to an earlier tradition about Aaluf, the brother of Horn, and King Silauf, who welcomed Aaluf. Mätzner has since published the text of *Horn* from the prints of its three MSS. in his *Altenglische Sprachproben*.
    Page 101. This Cotton fragment has the special value, says M. Paul Meyer, of preserving 140 lines, or parts of lines, of the beginning of the poem not in the Affleck and Cambridge MSS. The Cotton text is very close to the Affleck, as will be seen, for instance, by comparing our l. 191-209, p. 106-7, with l. 192-212, of Mr. David Laing's edition of the Affleck MS. for the Abbotsford Club. There are two editions of the French *Floris et Blancheflor*, by I. Bekker and M. du Méril. The poem in the *Romancero François* is a 'chanson,' p. 64, but at p. 57 is a short extract from the romance. P.M.—The German and Netherlandish complete editions are printed in Müller's *Sammlung* and in *Horæ Belgicæ*.

15. RELIGIOUS, POLITICAL, AND LOVE POEMS.—St. Gregory's Treutal. The late Mr. W. D. Turnbull printed a different Northern version of this from a 15th century MS. in the Advocate's Library (Jac. v. 7. 27), on p. 77-83 of his edition of *The Visions of Tundale*, etc., 1843. The scribe has wisely ended it with—
    " Be it trewe, or be it fals,
    It is as the copé was."
    Page 137, l. 642, *lore*: Dr. Stratmann says the short *o* of *lore* could not have rhymed with the long *o* of *more*. Accordingly, the Vernon text of the *Stacions*, p. 17, l. 522, reads *sore*.

23. AYENBITE OF INWYT.—Page 46, Sidenote to Sixth Head, *for* Foul (5 times) *read* Foolish, *as in Glossary*.

24. HYMNS TO THE VIRGIN.—Page 67, l. 288, *for* frere *read* frere.
    Page 96, l. 33. Is not the word rather to be read foonned (*n* NOT *u*)? = fonned = fond.—W. W. S.
    Page 127, l. 21, *for* cord *read* cors; l. 22, *for* fuly *the MS. reads* July.
    Page 132, col. 1. *Defie* is 'feel mistrust for;' see *Defier*, *Desfier*, in Cotgrave.—W. W. S.
    Page 137, col. 2. ȝeere.—To-ȝeere is a compound word, meaning *this year, soon;* see *To-year* in Halliwell: and I think with North Country men it is usual to say—You won't do it *t' year* (the year, this year) = You won't do it *in a hurry*. I'm convinced I've heard this phrase in some peasant's talk.—W. W. S.

25. CLENE MAYDENHOD.—Note to p. 7, destroy the comma after (Old High German).

PILGRIM'S SEA-VOYAGE.—Page 39. My guess is that *war-take* means simply *veering tackle*; the tackle whereby you *wear* the ship, or make it *veer*; or better still (as Mr. Hantler says), *take* = *tack*; and then *war* = wear, veer, *i.e.*, to *left* or *right*, just as he suggests.—W. W.S.

REPORT, 1867, p. 3, line 8 from foot. *Southern*.—Mr. R. Morris states that *Hali Meidenhad* as edited for the Society from the Nero MS. (but not in the Bodleian copy) has a large mixture of West Midland forms. See the Preface to his *Early English Homilies*, 1868, when issued.

28. PIERS PLOWMAN; TEXT A.—Page xxx. l. 16. For *rime-letter* read *chief-letter*, or *chief rime-letter*.

Page xxxvii. l. 8, from the bottom. The metrical dot should have been placed after *ffodis*.
Page 4, *foot-note to* l. 69. For *him*] DH *om*, read *him*] DH$_a$ *om*.
Page 5, l. 78. Insert the metrical dot after *he*.
Page 9, l. 43. Insert the same after *whom*.
Page 25, *foot-note to* l. 172. For wola loke II, *read* wole loke II.
Page 38, *foot-note to* l 192. For I batride on þe bak UD *read* I batride hym on þe bak UD.
Page 51, l. 154. For liue *read* lyue.
Page 68, *fourth side-note*. For cannot *read* cannot tell.
Page 75, *foot-note to* l. 29. For *see* U 221, 259, read *see* ll. 221, 259.
Page 79, l. 98. Insert the metrical dot after *pilgrimes*.
Page 80, l. 122. The initial letter is not illuminated; it should have been printed the same as the first letter in the next line.
Page 93, *footnote to* l. 26. Read *hem* (1)] hym T.
Page 99, *foot-note to* l. 135. For catonistris U *read* catonistris H.
Page 107, l. 80. *Read* þat þe [Erl] Auerous, etc. The word *Erl* should no doubt be inserted, though the Vernon MS. omits it.
Page 108, *foot-note to* l. 98. *The words* "him V." *belong to the end of the foot-note to* l. 96.
Page 113, *foot-note to* l. 62. The promised note to this line was accidentally omitted. It was merely intended to draw attention to the fact that the *omission* of the Latin words in MS. U is easily accounted for. They were to have been inserted in *red* letters, and a space was left for the purpose; but the illuminator forgot to insert them.
Page 126, *foot-note to* l. 79. For *see* ll. 73, etc., read *see* ll. 74, etc.
Page 139, l. 4. *For* 75 read 76.
Page 146, *note to* l. 68. *Add*, The quotation is from Ps. lxviii. 29 (Vulgate).
  "   *note to* l. 85. Transfer *heo*, so as to follow "have."
Page 153, l. 11 *from the bottom. Insert* the *in the vacant space. Three lines above*, commonded *should be* commended.

30. PIERCE THE PLOUGHMANS CREDE.—Page iii. line 14, *for* 1832 *read* 1842.
Page vi. l. 17, *read* specimens, *not* speciments.
Page 2, l. 26, *the word indistinctly printed is* holden.
Page 35, *add to note on* l. 65.—The Pied Friars had but one house, viz., at Norwich. We find the expression "Fratrum, quos *Freres Pye* veteres appellabant" in Thom. Walsingham, "Hist. Anglicana," vol. i. p. 182; ed. H. T. Riley.
Page 48, *note to* l. 516. *For* ther *read* þær; *and for* eah-thyrl *read* eah-þyrl.

32. BABEES BOOK, ETC.—Page 385, l. 5 from foot, *Read* v'sq. *versus*:

The publications of *The Early English Text Society* are divided into Four Classes. I. Arthur and other Romances. II. Works illustrating our Dialects and the History of our Language, including a Series of re-editions of our early Dictionaries. III. Biblical Translations and Religious Treatises. IV. Miscellaneous. The following are some of the works which in future years will be published in each of the Classes. (The *Extra Series*, commencing in 1867, is intended for re-editions.)

I.

Syr Thomas Maleore's Mort d'Arthur. To be edited from Caxton's edition (1485 A.D.) with a new Preface, Notes, and a Glossary. (*In the Extra Series*, 1868-9.)
The Romance of Arthour and Merlin. From the Auchinlech MS. (ab. 1320-30 A.D.), and the Lincoln's Inn and Douce MSS. (*In the Extra Series*.)
The History of the Saint Graal or Sank Ryal. By Henry Lonelich, Skynner (ab. 1440 A.D.). To be re-edited from the unique MS. in the Library of Corpus Christi Coll., Cambridge, by F. J. Furnivall, Esq., M.A. (*In the Extra Series*.)
The Arthur Ballads.
The Romance of Sir Tristrem. To be edited from the Auchinlech MS.
The English Charlemagne Romances. From the Auchinlech and other MSS.
The Romance of Sir Generides. From the MS. in Trin. Coll., Cambridge.
The Romance or Legend of Sir Ypotis. From the Vernon MS.

II.

Cursor Mundi, or Cursur o Worlde, in the Northern Dialect. To be edited from the MSS. in the British Museum and Trinity College, Cambridge, by R. Morris, Esq.
Hampole's Version of, and Commentary on, the Psalms. To be edited from a Northern MS. by R. Morris, Esq.
Hampole's other English Works in the Northern dialect.
The Gospel of Nicodemus in the Northumbrian dialect. To be edited for the first time from Harl. MS. 4196, etc., Cotton-Galba, E ix., by R. Morris, Esq.
Lives of Saints, in the Southern dialect. To be edited from the Harleian MS. 2277 (ab. 1305 A.D.), by R. Morris, Esq.
Barbour's Lives of Saints, in the Northern dialect. From the Cambridge University MS.
Catholicon Anglicum. To be edited from Lord Monson's MS., by H. B. Wheatley, Esq.
Abcedarium Anglico-latinum, pro Tyrunculis, Richardo Hulœto exscriptore. Londini, 1552.
A little Dictionary for Children (W. de Worde), or a shorte Dictionarie for yonge beginners (ed. Evans, 1566), by J. Withals. (The earliest edition to be collated with the succeeding editions.)
An Alvearie or Quadruple Dictionarie in Englishe, Latin, Greeke, and French, by John Baret. (The edition of 1580 collated with that of 1573.)
A Collection of Early English Treatises on Grammar. To be edited chiefly from MSS. for the first time by Henry B. Wheatley, Esq.

III.

The Old and New Testament in Verse. To be edited from the Vernon MS. by R. Morris, Esq.
The History of Adam and Eve. To be edited from the Vernon MS., Harl. MS. 1704, etc., by S. Wayland Kershaw, Esq., M.A.
The Stories of Susanna and the Elders, Lazarus, etc., To be edited from the Vernon MS., by J. W. Hales, Esq., M.A.
Medytacions of the Soper of our Lorde Ihesu, etc., perhaps by Robert of Brunne. To be edited from the Harl. MS. 1701 (ab. 1360 A.D.), etc., by F. J. Furnivall, Esq., M.A.
Lydgate's Life of St. Edmund. From the presentation MS. to Henry VI., Harl. 2278.

IV.

Two different Versions of Piers Plowman, in separate editions. To be edited from the MSS. by the Rev. W. W. Skeat, M.A.
Lydgate's Works.
Le Venery de Twety and The Master of the Game. To be edited from the MSS. by Alfred Sadler, Esq.
Barbour's Brus. To be edited from the MSS. in St. John's College, Cambridge, etc., by J. Peile, Esq., M.A., and the Rev. W. W. Skeat, M.A. (*In the Extra Series*, 1869).

Early English Text Society.

The Subscription is £1 1s. a year [and £1 1s. (Large Paper, £2 2s.) additional for the EXTRA SERIES], due in advance on the 1st of January, and should be paid either to the Society's Account at the Union Bank of London, 14, Argyll Place, Regent Street, W., or by post-office order (made payable to the Chief Office, London) to the Hon. Secretary, HENRY B. WHEATLEY, Esq., 53, Berners Street, London, W.

The Publications for 1867 are :—

24. HYMNS TO THE VIRGIN AND CHRIST; THE PARLIAMENT OF DEVILS; and other Religious Poems. Edited from the Lambeth MS. 853, by F. J. FURNIVALL, Esq., M.A. 3s.
25. THE STACIONS OF ROME, AND THE PILGRIMS' SEA-VOYAGE AND SEA-SICKNESS. WITH CLENE MAYDENHOD. Edited from the Vernon and Porkington MSS. etc., by F. J. FURNIVALL, Esq., M.A. 2s.
26. RELIGIOUS PIECES IN PROSE AND VERSE. Edited from ROBERT THORNTON'S MS. (ab. 1440 A.D.) by the Rev. G. G. PERRY, M.A. 2s.
27. LEVINS'S MANIPULUS VOCABULORUM, 1570; the earliest Rhyming Dictionary. Edited by HENRY B. WHEATLEY, Esq. 12s.
28. LANGLANDS' VISION OF PIERS PLOWMAN, with *Vita de Dowel, Dobet, et Dobest,* 1362 A.D. Part I. The earliest or Vernon Text; Text A. Edited from the Vernon MS., with full collations, by the Rev. W. W. SKEAT, M.A. 7s.
29. ENGLISH GILDS, their Statutes and Customs, with an Introduction and an Appendix of translated Statutes. Edited from the MSS. 1389 A.D., by TOULMIN SMITH, Esq.
30. PIERCE THE PLOUGHMAN'S CREDE. Edited from the MSS. by the Rev. W. W. SKEAT, M.A. 2s.

The Publications for 1868 will probably be—

31. MYRC'S INSTRUCTIONS FOR PARISH PRIESTS, in Verse. Edited for the first time from the MSS. in the British Museum and Bodleian Libraries (ab. 1420 A.D.) by E. PEACOCK, Esq. 4s.
32. THE BABEES BOKE, THE CHILDREN'S BOOK, URBANITATIS, THE BOKES OF NORTURE OF JOHN RUSSELL AND HUGH RHODES, THE BOKES OF KERUYNG, CORTASYE, AND DEMEANOUR, etc., with some French and Latin Poems on like subjects. Edited from Harleian and other MSS. by F. J. FURNIVALL, Esq., M.A. 15s.
33. THE KNIGHT DE LA TOUR LANDRY, 1372. A Father's Book for his Daughters. Edited from the Harleian MS. 1764, by THOMAS WRIGHT, Esq., M.A., and Mr. WILLIAM ROSSITER. 8s.
34. EARLY ENGLISH HOMILIES (ab. 1220-30 A.D.) from unique MSS. in the Lambeth and other Libraries. Edited by R. MORRIS, Esq. [*In the Press.*
35. MERLIN, Part III. Edited by H. B. WHEATLEY, Esq. [*In the Press.*

Among the Publications for 1869 will probably be :—

PALLADIUS ON HUSBONDRIE; the earliest English Poem on Husbandry. To be edited from the unique MS. in Colchester Castle (ab. 1425 A.D.) by the Rev. BARTON LODGE, M.A. Part I. [*In the Press.*
SIR DAVID LYNDESAY'S WORKS. Part III. To be edited by F. HALL, Esq., D.C.L.
EARLY SCOTTISH VERSE: MORAL AND HISTORICAL, from a MS. in the Cambridge University Library. To be edited by the Rev. J. R. LUMBY, M.A. [*In the Press.*
THE ALLITERATIVE ROMANCE OF THE DESTRUCTION OF TROY, translated from GUIDO DE COLONNA. To be edited from the unique MS. in the Hunterian Museum, Glasgow, by the Rev. G. A. PANTON. Part I. [*In the Press.*
VARIOUS POEMS RELATING TO SIR GAWAINE. To be edited from the MSS. by R. MORRIS, Esq.
RATIS RAVING, etc., a Collection of Scottish Prose and Verse on Moral and Religious Subjects. To be edited from a MS. in the Cambridge University Library, by the Rev. J. R. LUMBY, M.A.

EXTRA SERIES.

The Publications for 1867 (8vo., 1 guinea a year; Large Paper, 2 guineas) will be :—
I. GUILLAUME DE PALERNE; or, WILLIAM & THE WERWOLF. To be re-edited from the unique MS. in King's College, Cambridge, by the Rev. W. W. SKEAT, M.A.
II. CHAUCER'S PROSE WORKS. To be edited from the best MSS., with a Preface on the Grammar and Dialect of Chaucer and Notes, by RICHARD MORRIS, Esq. (the Rev. W. W. SKEAT assisting in the *Treatise on the Astrolabe*), and an Essay on the Pronunciation of Chaucer and Shakspere, by ALEXANDER J. ELLIS, Esq., F.R.S. Part I.

REPRINTING FUND.

When Thirty additional Subscribers' names are obtained, the Texts for 1864 will go to Press.

LONDON: N. TRÜBNER & CO., 60, PATERNOSTER ROW.
DUBLIN: WILLIAM McGEE, 18, NASSAU STREET.
EDINBURGH: T. G. STEVENSON, 22, SOUTH FREDERICK STREET.
GLASGOW: M. OGLE & CO., 1, ROYAL EXCHANGE SQUARE.
BERLIN: ASHER & CO., UNTER DEN LINDEN, 20.
NEW YORK: C. SCRIBNER & CO. LEYPOLDT & HOLT, 451, BROOME ST.
PHILADELPHIA: J. B. LIPPINCOTT & CO.
BOSTON, U.S.: DUTTON & CO.